FORGETTING
THE FORMER THINGS

FORGETTING
THE FORMER THINGS

Brain Injury's Invitation
to Vulnerability and Faith

Tamara Puffer

with

Joyce Hollyday

Foreword by Bill Gaventa

CASCADE *Books* · Eugene, Oregon

FORGETTING THE FORMER THINGS
Brain Injury's Invitation to Vulnerability and Faith

Cascade Books
An Imprint of Wipf and Stock Publishers
199 W. 8th Ave., Suite 3
Eugene, OR 97401

www.wipfandstock.com

PAPERBACK ISBN: 978-1-5326-5560-9
HARDCOVER ISBN: 978-1-5326-5561-6
EBOOK ISBN: 978-1-5326-5562-3

Cataloguing-in-Publication data:

Names: Puffer, Tamara, author. | Hollyday, Joyce, author. | Gaventa, Bill, foreword.

Title: Forgetting the former things : brain injury's invitation to vulnerability and faith / Tamara Puffer with Joyce Hollyday; foreword by Bill Gaventa.

Description: Eugene, OR: Cascade Books, 2019 | Includes bibliographical references.

Identifiers: ISBN 978-1-5326-5560-9 (paperback) | ISBN 978-1-5326-5561-6 (hardcover) | ISBN 978-1-5326-5562-3 (ebook)

Subjects: LCSH: Disabilities—Religious aspects—Christianity. | Providence and government of God—Christianity.

Classification: BT135 .P87 2019 (paperback) | CALL NUMBER (ebook)

Manufactured in the U.S.A.   01/18/19

Follow Tamara and Joyce in their blogs at:
Tamara: https://noggin-notions.com/
Joyce: https://joycehollyday.com/

To my husband, Michael Galovic

Contents

Foreword

In his book *The Wounded Storyteller*, sociologist Arthur Frank describes three cultural narratives that shape most of our responses to sudden and unexpected occurrences such as an accident or illness. The first is chaos, as trauma throws familiar frameworks of understanding and meaning into confusion. The second, most valued by Western societies and science, is recovery and healing: the miracle cure or surgery that pulls sufferers out of the great pit into which they have fallen and makes them "normal" again, as good as new. When such change does not occur, the reaction is often to move back to the first, living the chaos. But there is a third option. It is that of *journey*: a search for a "new normal" and for the sources of meaning that can sustain one through what will be a lifelong pilgrimage.

The words from Isaiah that give title to this book—and meaning to Tamara Puffer's journey from the point of impact in a life-changing car accident to the person she has become—are a perfect description of her very personal and particular journey, yet one that has universal implications. Tamara opens herself in *Forgetting the Former Things* for the rest of us to see and understand the ways in which her spirit, faith, and theology all shape, and have been shaped by, a traumatic brain injury. This is not a book about triumph over trauma with the help of faith. Rather, it is about tenacity, about the power of faith to mold and be molded by a long journey through a once-familiar landscape turned wilderness by the kind of event that could happen to any one of us.

That journey is not a straight line. It twists and turns, weaving in and out of new understandings as well as old memories of who Tamara was and is becoming. You see it in the titles of the chapters: "Rupture," "Rehabilitation," "Solidarity," "Wilderness," "Hope," "Broken," "Forward," "Crash," "Vulnerability," and "Healing."

Tamara's story feels utterly authentic to who she is and to her experience. For her, faith does not gloss over. It digs in, it despairs, it laughs, it tries, fails, and tries again, and it brings new understanding and meaning to commitments that have shaped her life from the beginning. Long called to ministry among the marginalized, she describes how she keeps putting herself in new margins—looking, one might say, for the new center of herself and the journey ahead.

The relative shortness of this book belies its depths. I am tempted to share the gems and flashes of light that all but took my breath away. But I will not. For you, the reader, will find your own. There is no fluff in Tamara's presentation of her experience and her biblical and theological reflections. They feel real, direct, true, and genuine. Thus, as a reader, like anyone who has the honor of listening to someone pour out their heart in a vulnerable place, you will walk away with gifts that can be used in your own search and struggle.

This faith story is not just about brain injury and those who are recovering from it. It is about all of us: how we all have to pick up the pieces, literally or figuratively, at some point in our lives. I would love to be part of a church circle, or a "fly on the wall" at a brain injury survivors group, where members read the book together and gather to talk about its meaning and impact for them.

I come back to the centrality of the Isaiah passage for Tamara's journey, and this "new thing" that God is building with God's people. Tamara takes a hard look at other parts of Isaiah that are often used to proclaim the redemptive and healing power of faith: "the deaf shall hear, the blind shall see, the lame will leap for joy." But she recognizes, with the help of Rabbi Julia Watts Belser, that such passages can be used in ways that are oppressive. When sufferers receive the message, either explicitly or implicitly, that cure will come if their faith is strong enough, self-blame is usually the result when it does not. The next step may be to believe that faith is worthless and people of faith are to be avoided. In my experience, that's been the story for so many persons with disabilities and their families.

There is, however, another image of recovery in Isaiah. In this one the people of Israel, including the disabled and injured ones, return to Jerusalem. All belong to the community and have the right as God's people to go home. I can easily imagine Tamara with them, back in the mostly destroyed city, rebuilding the wall and temple, using the ancient stones and materials where they can but also building something new.

Restoration means using the old and the new together for something newer still. The question is whether we have the faith, grit, and gumption to perceive it—and to keep building the city in which the God in each of us helps us flourish together. *Forgetting the Former Things* challenges, inspires, and helps to point the way forward.

Bill Gaventa, MDiv
Director, Summer Institute on Theology and Disability

Acknowledgments

In the years after I sustained a traumatic brain injury in a car accident in August 1996, I read a few books written by TBI survivors. After finishing each one, I said to myself, "I need to write a book." But I didn't pursue the thought. The idea intensified briefly when I attended my first Summer Institute on Theology and Disability (SITD), held in Toronto in 2013. But there, among theologians and practitioners, I decided I couldn't write an academic book and pushed it out of my mind one more time.

Then, at the following year's Summer Institute in Dallas, I spoke to SITD faculty member John Swinton, who is the director of the Centre for Spirituality, Health and Disability at the University of Aberdeen in Scotland. "I really want to write something about brain injury with some theological reflection," I told him. "I haven't seen anything like that written by a TBI survivor. But I don't even know where to start."

John's response was, "Find somebody to work with you." I filed that thought away. But my brain's filing system (memory) isn't what it used to be before the car accident, with ideas relatively easy for me to store but often difficult to retrieve. So I forgot—until I mentioned my hope of writing a book to Bill Gaventa, the director of SITD. His response was virtually identical to John's: "Well, you could always work with someone."

So, with their encouragement, I got serious about trying to find someone to help me write a book. I'm a Presbyterian minister, active at Grace Covenant Presbyterian Church in Asheville, North

Carolina, and also at Circle of Mercy, a congregation affiliated with the United Church of Christ and the Alliance of Baptists that gathers on Sunday evenings. Months went by, and then one Sunday night during the worship service, it occurred to me that I could ask Joyce Hollyday, one of the founders of Circle of Mercy. When I was serving a church near Atlanta and she was an editor of *Sojourners* magazine, I read her columns and other writings. I considered her something of a celebrity and doubted she would work with me.

I had first met Joyce when she moved to Atlanta to attend Emory University's Candler School of Theology in 1995. I remember thinking, "She doesn't have a seminary degree? My word, she knows more theology than I do. I wouldn't want to be her professor!" Back then we were both volunteers at the Open Door Community, serving prisoners and people living on the streets. We got to know each other as I rode with her once a month to the prison in Jackson, Georgia, for visits with men on death row. I don't know what I expected, but it wasn't who Joyce was at all. I was surprised then by how accessible and down-to-earth she was, and I thought maybe I'd be surprised again. I decided to ask for her help.

She didn't hesitate at all. Her "yes" was great news. But it immediately made me doubt whether I could actually write a book. I have challenges with organization, focus, and stamina. The longest pieces I've written since my accident are sermons, and pulling them off takes me a long time. I also experience what is called "flooding": ideas come to me in no particular order, and I am easily overwhelmed. I really needed someone to help provide a theological framework as well as organize my scattered thoughts.

Joyce and I began working together in June 2015. As the months went by, my doubts deepened. "I can't do this," I often said to her. And in her measured way, she always responded, "I know you can, Tamara. I wouldn't work with you if I didn't think you have something to say." So I kept writing, even though I wondered whether the money I was paying her for a few hours of planning, coaching, and editing each week would ever pay off.

The game changed when Joyce suggested that I apply for a Pastoral Studies Grant from the Lilly Endowment-funded

Louisville Institute. She helped me fill out the long application, and in my usually negative way, I figured I had no chance. I decided that when my request was declined, I would stop working on the book. But to my surprise, I received a grant. Without it, *Forgetting the Former Things* would not have been written.

Joyce and I met weekly, with her giving me assignments to write. I contacted my parents, Keith and Donna Puffer, and my sister, Lori Puffer, who live in Kansas City, to help fill in the details of my recovery, some of which I missed while in a coma. I also got in touch with Rev. Dr. Carol Strickland—who was the associate pastor at Mount Vernon Presbyterian Church, where I was working when the accident happened—who visited me several times while I was in the hospital.

The passing of time and my memory issues meant that piecing together the story was difficult. I imagine it wasn't easy for my family and friends to relive those events, and I appreciate their willingness, because I could not have done it without them. Details may have become blurry for all of us over two decades, and I apologize if there are any inaccuracies in these pages. But they don't alter the core truth of the story, which we reconstructed to the best of our collective ability.

At several points I agonized about whether this book was any good, so Joyce suggested that I give the completed early chapters to several folks for their opinions. I chose friends, pastors, and a fellow brain injury survivor: Dale Roberts, Cathy Walgenbach, Suzie Churchfield, Carl Griffith, Nancy Hastings Sehested, Sarah Gualtieri, and Mark Ramsey. Their positive comments gave me the energy to continue, and I'm grateful that they took the time to read the manuscript while it was in process.

I went through a personal transformation writing this book. I first thought Joyce would simply edit my work. After several months, it became painfully clear that I needed her to do more than edit. I believe Joyce came to that conclusion as well but didn't want to hurt me by telling me. Realizing my limitations caused a great internal struggle, but through the process I learned that it's okay to need help. Reflections on vulnerability and interdependence became a much larger part of the story on these pages than I had ever imagined.

Over the years I have heard many stories of TBI survivors receiving inadequate medical, professional, and mental health services. This was not the case for me, and for that I am very thankful. Without the competent intervention of a multitude of care providers—from emergency technicians to physicians to therapists of all stripes—I likely would not have survived, and surely would not have reached the point of being able to write this book.

Finally, I want to thank my husband, Michael Galovic. He has been amazing. He has supported me from Day One of my recovery, when he faced the scary possibility that I would not remember him after emerging from my coma. While my medical providers and rehabilitation staff were wonderful, he certainly kept them on their toes.

Michael put up with my various moods as I worked on writing this book. Many days I was depressed, and if you have ever been around a depressed person, you know it isn't easy. He's certainly not perfect, for which I am grateful, because I needed someone around me willing to share his weaknesses. This gave me the courage to face my own challenges. One of Michael's best gifts to me is that he is a former CPA who thinks like a CPA. He is extremely well organized, and he offered solutions for the many challenges we faced. And to top it all off, he formatted this book for me.

I regret that I probably missed the names of some folks who've helped me with *Forgetting the Former Things*. Please know that I am grateful to you as much as I appreciate everyone I have mentioned above.

Tamara Puffer
Asheville, NC
March 6, 2018

* * *

I simply want to add a note of thanks to Tamara for giving me the honor of working with her on her compelling story. My style when coaching authors is to lay out options and provide gentle guidance on the writing journey. Early in our process, on more than one occasion, Tamara uttered some version of "Just tell me what to do." When I finally grasped how overwhelming sorting through possibilities felt to her, I dug deep to find my "inner tyrant" and began more intentionally shaping this book and assigning her pieces to write. So the story is hers, but any errors in organization or emphasis are mine.

That lesson was the first of many I learned about the day-to-day challenges of brain injury. Before working with Tamara, I probably would have said that I was blind to this reality and had my eyes opened through the process of working with her. But among the most important lessons for me was coming to understand how I/we use language that is offensive to persons with disabilities, too often employing the terms "blindness," "deafness," and "paralysis" when referring to moral failures such as ignorance, apathy, and hardheartedness.

I spent a lot of time trying to second-guess how I could be most helpful to Tamara in a variety of situations, from attending a Louisville Institute consultation to preaching a sermon together at Circle of Mercy and co-facilitating a workshop at the 2017 Summer Institute on Theology and Disability near Los Angeles. I finally figured out that the appropriate strategy was to ask her. She taught me how to take seriously her disability and the limitations it imposes, and at the same time see her as far more than her brain injury. She has been a patient teacher, opening up intimate glimpses of her world to me with warmth and grace.

Working with Tamara over a span of three years enabled me to see her at her best and her worst—as she saw me in those extremes as well. I am simply amazed at her persistence, courage, and strength of character, as she continued to unravel her often-painful story in the face of bouts of depression and daily struggles

Acknowledgments

with energy and focus. I am inspired by both the vulnerability and the power she reveals on these pages.

Unforgettable is the pot of tea that Tamara bought for me to sip while we shared an hour at a teahouse near her home about halfway through the writing process. It was South African Rooibos Masala tea, mixed with warm milk and Appalachian honey, infused with hints of cinnamon, cardamom, ginger, cloves, and orange peel—savored with a strong dose of triumph. It was my payoff for winning a bet. Tamara had been convinced that the early readers of her manuscript would not see value in her book; I was equally convinced that they would be enthusiastic.

I rejoice and give thanks that our friendship, which began more than two decades ago in Atlanta, has deepened through the challenges and delights of working together to create *Forgetting the Former Things*. I also thank my surprise late-in-life partner, Bill Ramsey, and Circle of Mercy pastors Nancy Hastings Sehested and Missy Harris for their care and support at critical points along this journey.

Joyce Hollyday
Marshall, NC
April 3, 2018

Introduction

Do not fear,
for I have redeemed you;
I have called you by name,
You are mine.
When you pass through the
waters, I will be with you;
and through the rivers, they
shall not overwhelm you;
when you walk through fire you
shall not be burned,
and the flame shall not consume you . . .

Do not remember the former things,
or consider the things of old.
I am about to do a new thing;
now it springs forth;
do you not perceive it?
I will make a way in the wilderness
and rivers in the desert.
(Isa 43:1–2, 18–19)

On the afternoon of September 20, 2016, I was at my home in Asheville, North Carolina, writing a section of this book. One hundred and thirty miles away in Charlotte, a police officer fatally shot Keith Lamont Scott while he was waiting in the parking lot at his apartment complex for his son to return home from school. The killing prompted three nights of protest, a declaration of a state of emergency by our governor, and a call to the National Guard to back up police, who employed tear gas and rubber bullets when the largely nonviolent protests grew confrontational. By the time it was over, several people were injured and another man was dead.

Reports conflict describing Mr. Scott's killing, from his wife Rakeyia Scott, other eyewitnesses, and the police officers on the scene. Available video footage is inconclusive on the details in dispute. But what is clear from the record on Ms. Scott's cellphone is that she said to the police repeatedly, "Don't shoot him. He has no weapon."

Officers continued yelling, "Drop the gun!" Ms. Scott repeated her pleas. "He doesn't have a gun!" she shouted. "He has a TBI. He's not going to do anything to you guys. He just took his medicine." When Mr. Scott got out of his vehicle and began backing away from it, a police officer opened fire and killed him.

The tragedy raised strong emotions in me: anger, frustration, grief. I wondered, did those officers even know that a TBI is a traumatic brain injury? Did they have any understanding that a person with a TBI in such a stressful situation would feel disoriented and act in ways that might seem unusual?

Keith Lamont Scott had sustained a brain injury in a motorcycle accident, in which he also broke both his hips and his nose, in November 2015. Afterward, according to his family, he had difficulty with speech and memory. In the aftermath of his killing, Susan H. Connors, president and CEO of the Brain Injury Association of America, released a statement to the press. It said in part: "Traumatic brain injury can result in problems with receptive language, or understanding what is being said, and individuals may have a delayed reaction to commands. It is important that public officials and first responders throughout the country come to understand the complexities involved with brain injury."[1]

I have wished for greater understanding of brain injury ever since the August 1996 car accident that changed my life. I'm heartened that brain injury and other cognitive disabilities have recently appeared in the national spotlight. But I'm saddened that this increased attention has come largely as a result of all the TBIs

---

1. Connors, Brain Injury Association.

suffered by veterans of the Iraq and Afghanistan wars injured by IEDs (improvised explosive devices); the revelation of widespread CTE (chronic traumatic encephalopathy) among football players; and the epidemic of Alzheimer's disease and other forms of dementia among our elders.

As a Presbyterian pastor, I've paid attention to how often brain injury survivors and their families in the support groups I've attended have spoken about feeling uncomfortable in church. Most have found that stating their needs is difficult, and their injuries are frequently misunderstood. The 1990 Americans with Disabilities Act launched a round of conversations and study that placed the issue of disability squarely into the life of the church. Many local churches began to address accessibility with heightened resolve. But I was left wondering: What about the concerns that can't be solved with an elevator or a wheelchair ramp? What about the "invisible" reality of cognitive disability? What about the many people who leave our churches feeling hurt and misunderstood, who have been treated as charity cases or objects of pity, receiving offers of help but never invitations to offer their gifts?

Recent years have brought an increase in books about theology and disability, but few address brain injury and other cognitive challenges. Those that do are written almost exclusively by researchers, observers, or caregivers. I wrestled for a few years over whether to write this book. It was not easy. The process of writing highlighted my cognitive deficits, pushed the limits of my stamina, and drained my patience. I don't remember everything that happened to me around my accident. Focusing on what I can recall and recording the traumas of that moment, my long rehabilitation, and my ongoing losses raised a mountain of emotions.

But I'm glad that I persisted. My connection with other brain injury survivors, and the responses I've received to my blogs, articles, and sermons, have convinced me that the need is great for sharing experiences and engaging in public conversation about the growing reality of brain injury and its impact on the church and our culture more broadly. I hope that *Forgetting the Former Things* will contribute to that ongoing conversation.

There's a saying in the brain injury community: "If you know one person with a brain injury . . . you know one person with a brain injury." I decided to write this book about my experience in part because I can. So many others with brain injuries have lost that ability, landing at a different place on the broad spectrum of function. I don't claim to speak for them, but I hope that my personal and theological reflection in these pages can be a lens through which they and those around them can understand their struggles and triumphs, helping to move brain injury further out of the realm of invisibility.

This book is intended for brain injury survivors, their partners and families, and the pastors, teachers, and medical professionals who serve them. It is also for all the people who feel that their life hasn't turned out the way they had envisioned it: for all those who have suffered the rupture of illness or divorce, the loss of a job or the unexpected death of a loved one.

I have given it the title *Forgetting the Former Things*. When I was coming out of a two-week induced coma after my accident, two verses from my favorite Old Testament prophet, Isaiah, ran repeatedly through my mind: "Do not remember the former things, or consider the things of old. I am about to do a new thing." The book title is a double entendre that speaks of the forgetting and memory challenges that result from brain injury, and the need to let go of what once was in order to be open to reimagining one's life.

I've come a long way. And, in many ways, I'm still waiting to see what "new thing" is around the next corner. I cling to Isaiah's promise that God has claimed, redeemed, and called me by name. God is leading me through a wilderness, making a path that isn't always clear to me. But I have not been overwhelmed or consumed. I have not been abandoned. And I need not fear.

1

Rupture

August 26, 1996. Monday morning. The alarm jolts me awake at 4:15. I reach over and turn it off, weary from the previous day's worship and youth group responsibilities. Michael, my husband of three months, lies still. I wish I could stay beside him for a while longer on my day off, at least until the sun comes up. He has the luxury of sleeping while I make my way in the dark into downtown Atlanta.

Once I'm out the door, I always look forward to these early Monday mornings with the Open Door Community. It's where Michael and I met fourteen months ago, when he was a resident volunteer and I showed up one day with my church youth group to help out with the soup kitchen. In the spirit of the Catholic Worker tradition of hospitality, the Open Door welcomes people off the streets into its life and, with a throng of volunteers, provides services including meals, showers, and clean clothes.

As always, one-eyed Ralph Dukes is waiting to greet me with his toothless smile, awake before everyone else to start the coffee. I turn on the heat to hard-boil twenty dozen eggs and stir a massive pot of grits on the industrial stove. Ralph removes huge trays of sliced oranges from the refrigerator. Before long, the kitchen fills up with an array of sleepy humanity. We load up the food, bowls, spoons, and mugs into a van and head toward Butler Street AME Church.

A couple hundred people are huddled in front of the church. Some of the men need a quick and hearty breakfast before standing among the crowds at the day-labor pools, hoping against hope to get chosen for a few hours of minimum-wage work. But most of the folks waiting have nowhere to go and nothing to do but wander the streets for rest of the day.

I think, as I often do on Monday mornings, of Jesus' words recorded in the Gospel of Matthew: "Truly I tell you, just as you did it to one of the least of these who are members of my family, you did it to me" (Matt 25:40, NRSV). Jesus was speaking of feeding the hungry, clothing the poor, welcoming the stranger, visiting the sick and imprisoned—those deemed "least" in the eyes of the world but precious to him. He was telling his followers where to find him, who he claimed as family, and how to minister to his hurting sisters and brothers. His command of unconditional compassion has been turning my theology inside out.

As I ladle up the grits, I can't help noting the dramatic contrast between the precarious lives filing before me and the members of the affluent suburban church where I serve as an associate pastor. Some of the folks from the streets drink or use illegal drugs to escape their pain. I know that some of the people in the church I serve also struggle with drugs and alcohol, but their financial situations usually allow them to keep these issues hidden. I wonder where some of the men and women from the Butler Street breakfast would be if they had been born to wealthier parents, or if they had other people in their lives that cared more about them. I recognize, uncomfortably, that my financial security, relational stability, and high degree of formal education mean that I have much more in common with the members of my church than these friends living on the streets.

Under the influence of Scripture, Michael, the Open Door, and my own questioning spirit, my understanding of Jesus is expanding. I yearn to know more deeply this One who lived his life on the margins, from birth in a stable to execution on a criminal's cross. Who was this Jesus who proclaimed that he had come to "bring good news to the poor" (Luke 4:18); who befriended the outcasts and spurned those in power; who announced the coming of a new day with the words "Blessed are you who are poor, for yours is the kingdom of God" (Luke 6:20)? And how can I respond to the call that is growing in me to serve and learn from those who now make their home with him on the margins?

* * *

By 9 o'clock we're back at the Open Door, with all the dishes washed and stacked in their cupboards. The rest of the day passes quietly and unremarkably at home. Michael and I grab a quick dinner and decide to drive to a nearby TCBY and treat ourselves to some frozen yogurt. On short jaunts like this we often bring our dog Abu, a playful Lhasa Apso mix with a fringe of gray fur over her eyes, but we agree to leave her at home this time.

My usual order at TCBY is a cup of chocolate yogurt swirled with white chocolate mousse. Between bites, sitting on the street-level ledge of a building on busy Roswell Road, I begin to share with Michael my hopes and fears about a phone interview coming up later in the week. It's for an associate pastor position in a church where I would have more responsibility and serve people more in line with my calling to ministry among the marginalized.

I've already had one phone interview and am excited about the invitation to have a second. But I have misgivings. I wonder aloud how I would be able to come up with a sermon every week, when it takes me so long to write the two sermons a year I preach now. True to character, I'm already worrying about a job that I haven't even been offered.

Encouraged that I've been invited for a second interview, Michael assures me that I preach well and that sermon preparation will get easier the more I do it. A fan of Heath Bar topping on whatever flavor yogurt he gets, he finishes up the last crunchy remnant, stands up to throw away his cup and napkin, and says, "I hope you get the job. But if you do, I'll have to figure out what I'm going to do."

Michael is a free-spirited kind of guy, which is one reason I was attracted to him. He worked as a successful accountant in Indiana before realizing that his life was feeling restricted and not as fulfilling as he wanted it to be. So in his late twenties, he dropped everything and moved to Cocoa Beach, Florida, to live by the ocean. There he met new friends and became active in a Catholic young-adult group that provided him with needed fellowship as he began seeking a new lifestyle and career.

He's now working two very-part-time jobs. Our plan is for me to serve a church where I can develop my preaching, pastoral care, and urban ministry skills and at the same time support Michael while he pursues further education, perhaps a PhD in anthropology, which is a growing interest. We have a broad outline but lack the specifics.

Michael is driving as we leave the TCBY. Our car, recently purchased, has a manual transmission that I haven't yet mastered. It's rush hour, and Roswell Road is packed. As we near home, I remember a prescription I have waiting at the Drug Emporium and suggest that we pick it up.

Michael eases into the left-turn lane in the center of the road. A car, large and recognizable as a Cadillac, is approaching. But it's far enough away that Michael decides he has time to make the turn. He puts our car into what he thinks is first gear and presses the gas pedal while letting up on the clutch.

The car lurches and then haltingly stutters forward. I scream as the Cadillac bears down, coming straight at me. The slam rattles every bone in my body, as the sound of crashing metal fills the early evening air. Then everything goes blank and silent.

***

I miss two weeks of my existence, kept in an induced coma in an Atlanta trauma hospital to guard against brain swelling.

Although unable to fully comprehend it at the time, I wake up to a different life.

Slowly, over time, Michael, my family members, and friends unravel the details of the harrowing minutes, hours, and days after the accident. Michael remembers being startled back to consciousness by the sound of someone pounding on the car window. His hands were locked at the ten and two positions on the steering wheel. He called to me, "Hey, Tamara, wake up!" When I didn't respond, he said to himself, *Okay, I'll let her sleep. But I'm going to get out of the car.*

He opened the door and stepped out. Someone on the scene told him that his ear was bleeding and suggested that he take off his shirt and use it to put pressure there. Michael complied. And then he said, matter-of-factly, "You know, I'm tired. I'm going to lie down." He stretched out on his back in the grass by the side of the road and lost consciousness again.

Members of the Emergency Medical Team brought him back. They began talking to him in gentle tones. "Okay, we're going to move your head now." "We're putting a neck brace on you; it doesn't mean that anything is wrong." "Now we're going to put you on the stretcher." Though in other circumstances he might have judged their words excessive, in that moment he experienced them as comfort.

After they got Michael settled in an ambulance, a police officer approached and dropped a traffic ticket into his lap. Then the ambulance door slammed. That's when understanding jolted Michael's mind like a thunderbolt. He began praying fervently that I would be okay. As he was whisked off to nearby Northside Hospital, I was rushed unconscious to the trauma center at Dunwoody Medical Center.

We had no family in Atlanta, and Michael was concerned that the staff at Mount Vernon Presbyterian Church should know that I wasn't going to be showing up for work the next day. He gave the name and phone number of my pastoral colleague as our emergency contact. Someone from the hospital called Carol Strickland

and, lacking any contact information for my family in Kansas City, she tried to locate them.

Fortunately, my rather unusual last name made the task relatively easy. Carol called the first "Puffer" she came across in the phone book. The person who answered was my ninety-one-year-old grandfather, who suffered from dementia. Carol wisely chose not to share the news with him. On the second try, she reached my parents.

They caught the first flight from Kansas City to Atlanta the next morning. My sister Lori stayed behind to run the three family-owned transmission shops. My mother remembers sitting in the waiting room outside my ICU, talking Lori through fulfilling payroll. All their employees got paid on time.

Dad called Lori every day with updates. He always tries to put a positive spin on things, but my sister could hear the quiver in his voice when he spoke. A physician's assistant at the hospital familiar with my case told Mom, "She isn't going to make it." A nurse friend sitting with my mother was livid at the insensitivity of the comment.

Michael, having sustained a fractured skull and a mild brain injury, spent five days at Northside Hospital. When Elizabeth Dede and Gladys Rustay from the Open Door Community paid a visit, he was lying on his back holding his head. They walked in the door and greeted him in unison, "Hey, Michael!" He lifted his head to look at them and promptly threw up. The nurse said sensitively, "Nausea is very common with brain trauma," as she mopped up the mess.

Michael's brother, Bob, drove up from Florida the day after the accident and stayed for a couple of days, visiting both of us in our respective hospitals. Michael's mother drove from Indiana with his Aunt Loretta two days later and stayed for a week in our apartment. I still shudder to think about the state they found it in. Neither Michael nor I is terribly interested in housekeeping, and I imagine the two women discovered some work to do—though, graciously, they never mentioned it.

As I talked later to my family and friends about that time, I began to understand how terrifying all the uncertainty was for them. "If someone tries to tell you they know what will happen, they're lying," a physician said to Michael one day while he waited outside the ICU to visit me. There's simply no way of knowing at that stage what will be recovered and what has been lost forever.

What Michael remembers most is being really, really tired. For several weeks he felt unable to function. He compared himself to the disciples at Gethsemane the night before Jesus died. Jesus had asked them to stay awake while he prayed, anticipating Judas's betrayal and the soldiers' arrest. But his closest friends kept falling asleep. Michael felt like he was betraying me by nodding off at the hospital as he waited to visit while I lay in a coma in the ICU. But of course it had nothing to do with betrayal. We've since learned that overwhelming fatigue is very common in brain injury survivors as the brain heals.

My sister Lori and my grandmother flew to Atlanta on Labor Day weekend. The medical staff encouraged them to talk to me, assuring them that I could hear them even though I was non-responsive. Lori later reflected that "it felt kind of funny talking to someone lying there looking like she was in a fight and lost."

Attached to my skull was a metal bolt that monitored the blood pressure inside my brain. Had it become dangerously high, my doctor would have done surgery to release the pressure. Fortunately, that didn't happen. At one point, he asked Michael if it was okay to insert a feeding tube in me. It was a simple procedure, but it carried risks. That's when Michael realized how foggy his brain was and how briefly he had known me. With my parents' blessing, he approved the procedure.

When I was finally conscious and stable, I was moved by ambulance to North Fulton Hospital, which has an inpatient unit for brain injury rehabilitation. It was September twelfth, my parents' wedding anniversary. They shared their anniversary dinner with Michael in the hospital cafeteria.

As is common with brain injury survivors, my bed was enveloped by a zippered soft mesh cage, which allowed me to thrash around without hurting myself. My colleague Carol told me later that visiting me was awkward, as I was nonverbal and my face looked rather "wild," lacking the composure people normally have. Once I threw off my shirt. Though I was embarrassed when she told me, I later learned that this is fairly typical behavior for someone at that stage of healing.

At first Carol carried on a one-way conversation or just sat quietly. Sometimes she sang the "Doxology" and "Gloria Patri," knowing how much I love music. As I healed, I eventually joined Carol in singing the hymns, grateful for the connection between music and memory.

About a month after the accident, Michael took our car to the Jiffy Lube near where it had happened. The man behind the counter recognized him. "You were in that car accident, weren't you?"

"Yeah, that was me," Michael answered.

The clerk went on to talk about how bad it had looked, how traffic was stopped way up Roswell Road and he and his employees couldn't even get out of their parking lot. "I'm glad you're okay," he said. He stopped then and looked tentatively at Michael before asking, "What happened to the woman you were with?"

Michael told him that I was out of the ICU and getting rehabilitation therapy, doing better.

"Oh, I'm so glad!" said the man behind the counter, looking both surprised and relieved. "We were sure she had died."

2

Rehabilitation

Michael still had no idea what was in store for us. Doctors at North Fulton again reminded him of the uncertainty of brain injury recovery. One said that there was no way of knowing what I would remember, and that often older memories remain while newer ones fade. Michael, painfully aware of how new our marriage was, was very worried that I wouldn't remember him.

I still have the "memory log" that was kept for me when I began my rehabilitation at North Fulton's Renaissance Rehabilitation Center. Since I was unable to do it myself, my therapists wrote in the log every day. Each page lists the following therapies: physical, occupational, speech, recreational, and cognitive. Nurses and family members also made notations about my progress.

Someone wrote the names of the staff members working with me on a page, next to Polaroid pictures of each of them. Though I don't remember a lot about my early weeks in rehab, seeing their photographs always gives me a good feeling. Sometimes the body remembers what the mind cannot.

The first staff notation describes my initial speech therapy session, on September seventeenth: "Worked on pointing to common objects on command and on using the objects appropriately." Apparently my speech therapist and I also reviewed body parts. Odd as it may sound, being unable to tell a hand from a foot is a common result of brain injury. In a few days an occupational therapist was going to help me dress myself, and I needed to know the difference.

Before I could even attempt dressing, I first had to regain strength in my arms. So the second day I tossed bean bags and reviewed body parts again. I don't know what my particular challenges were in this area, but it's typical for brain injury survivors not to know what article of clothing to put on first, often making errors like putting underwear over pants.

One day a therapist held up a pen and asked me what it was. I quickly responded, "Banana parts!" Michael stifled his laughter. But the therapist said, "You're close. It's a ballpoint pen." She explained that my brain had probably made a connection between the first letters of each word. Every wisp of encouragement helped.

Michael later described my physical therapy sessions to me. "At first, the physical therapists took you by the armpits and carried you, pretending like you were walking," he reported. On September nineteenth they were carrying me to the door. He remembers that I grabbed the knob, turned to him, and quietly whispered, "Michael."

"Did you hear that?" the therapist asked excitedly. "She called your name!" This was apparently a relief to her—and certainly to Michael. This moment, three weeks after the accident, was his first indication that I remembered him.

Michael was very involved in my care during rehab. He asked a lot of questions, which some of my treatment providers appreciated and others found annoying. When I asked him later about that time, he said, "I know I was really protective. I was demanding toward your treatment staff. Looking back on it, I was probably kind of a jerk."

My parents also supported me with their presence but, to my chagrin, I have no memory of their visits. I do, however, remember that Michael brought our dog, Abu, for a visit once—a delightful break in the routine. Apart from them, Michael limited visitors, in order to minimize my stress and fatigue.

During my six weeks in the rehab hospital, I spent my days playing catch with a football and riding a stationary bicycle. I walked up steps and alongside a balance beam, until I could get around with the help of a cane. My log shows that I regained physical movement by leaps and bounds. I also repeated words over and over. Michael noted that by October fifth, my birthday, I was speaking clearly, with about 90 percent of my vocabulary restored.

One day a nurse asked me if I wanted some coffee. I told her, "I don't drink coffee."

That was totally untrue. I'm actually somewhat of a coffee snob. After I graduated from seminary, before accepting the call to my church position, I worked in an upscale coffee store in an Atlanta shopping mall. I enjoyed it and learned how to make a mean cappuccino.

Michael had been trying to get me to quit drinking coffee for quite some time. He silently gave thanks that this part of my memory had disappeared. But, to his disappointment, eventually it came back and I remembered how much I enjoyed coffee and took up drinking it again.

At the rehab hospital, my speech therapist recognized that I had double vision, caused by damage during the accident to the nerves that operate my eye muscles. She made a removable eye patch for me out of black poster board and Velcro, which fastened over my glasses. She instructed me to wear it every day, one day over my right eye and the next day over the left, to strengthen both.

As soon as I was able to write a little, I began jotting down lists in a journal. I could only print, barely legibly. Because I couldn't yet formulate sentences and complicated thoughts, I made a lot of lists. Typical of my entries, one day I wrote:

Perhaps I'll list the things I need to work on. I may forget some of them.

1. *Speech*
2. *Vision: I must wear a patch*
3. *Use of right hand*
4. *Speech*

5. *Memory. I especially want to remember dates and names.*

6. *Use of physical body. My use of the right hand is horrible.*

I find it funny that right after I listed speech for a second time, I listed memory. My right hand was obviously a concern as well.

* * *

When the time came for me to be discharged from the hospital, Michael and I had to choose which of two available centers would continue my rehab. Since thinking through that decision was beyond my capacities at the time, Michael had to make it on his own. He found the process agonizing, carrying the burden of believing that the selection would make or break my recovery and determine whether or not I would heal enough to be able to return to ministry. Always organized, he kept a notebook and made a list of the pros and cons for each of the two facilities. Our insurance company assured him that, if we encountered a problem at whichever one he chose, he could move me to the other.

Michael wanted me to come home and receive outpatient rehab. My treatment team felt strongly that I needed to be in a residential program. But initially our insurance company agreed only to pay for outpatient treatment. So, hoping for the best, Michael moved me to Meadowbrook rehabilitation center, which generously gave me the first night's stay free of charge while we waited for a final determination. Thankfully, the insurance company approved residential care for me the next day.

I have only vague impressions of my time at Meadowbrook. It consisted of two small buildings. My room was on the second floor of the main building, which had a kitchen, physical therapy room, and computer lab downstairs. Building on the work I had begun at North Fulton, I had an hourly schedule of therapies and full days of rehabilitation. One notation in my journal indicates that my therapists kept me very busy but gave me frequent breaks due to my fatigue.

I especially liked music therapy, which meant that I got to sing. Probably nothing did more to reconnect me to myself during that time than music. Before becoming a pastor, I had made a living as a professional musician, violin and viola teacher, and church choir director. Voice and violin had shaped my life from an early age, and singing tapped into my deep love of music.

Occasionally the therapists took some of us from Meadowbrook to a nearby shopping mall or restaurant, to get us used to being in crowds again. Sometimes we went to a YMCA for recreational therapy. Michael was present the first time and was amazed that I "swam like a fish." I remember that I loved being in the pool, because there my physical limitations disappeared; I didn't need a cane to swim laps.

I saw no choice but to pray and hope for the best—and work very, very hard to recover what I'd lost. Michael and I assumed that I would learn to walk, speak, eat, and think clearly again. And then, according to our plan, I would go back into the "call process," the method through which Presbyterian pastors find a new position. Before long I would be serving another church and supporting Michael while he went to graduate school.

Back then reading was difficult, and so I didn't read anything, including my Bible. But I vividly recall the comforting words from Isaiah coming to mind on nights that I had trouble falling asleep: "Do not remember the former things or consider the things of old. I am about to do a new thing . . . "

I remember thinking that I was going to ignore the "Do not consider the things of old" part; it seemed important to integrate the past into one's present. But I also knew that what I needed most was a word of hope for my future. *My speech will improve. I will go home. I will be a minister again. God is doing a new thing. I simply must wait.*

* * *

Toward the end of my month at Meadowbrook, I was allowed a couple of short visits at home. I was excited when I realized that soon I would be home for good with Michael, sleeping in a familiar bed. But making a visit meant that I had to ride in a car, a prospect that was very scary. When Michael came to get me for the first home visit, I climbed into the back seat and made him drive me around like a chauffeur. Several months passed before I felt safe enough to sit in the passenger's seat beside him.

I have little memory of the home visits, although I do recall wandering around our apartment, trying to get reoriented to it, with Abu trotting along behind me. In late October I was discharged as an inpatient from Meadowbrook. On our first Thanksgiving together as a married couple, Michael and I were bestowed with a meal lovingly prepared by a former chef from my church—a traditional feast of turkey with all the trimmings. It was a delightful day.

We were a pair to behold. In the months after the accident, Michael sometimes had mild dizzy spells related to his brain injury, which seemed to be worse after dark. I had regained most of my balance during physical therapy, spending long stretches standing on one foot and then the other, staring at a spot on the wall—but I couldn't see well, especially at night. So sometimes the two of us groped our way through the dark, Michael leaning on my arm to steady himself, issuing verbal instructions: "There's a step down"; "The pavement turns here"; "Be careful of the rock up ahead." It was a case of "the visually challenged leading the physically unbalanced"—a scenario I hadn't imagined for us for at least a few more decades. We tried to laugh about it.

I continued my therapy at Meadowbrook as an outpatient, but by December I was very frustrated. I couldn't understand how the activities I was assigned were helping me to get back to work. Many days I played Hangman in the computer lab. I don't remember anyone explaining to me that this exercise was designed to boost my vocabulary. I thought Hangman was a nice little game, but it seemed like a waste of time. *How*, I wondered, *could it possibly help me return to ministry?* The closest I came to church work was the hours I spent painting a ceramic replica of Noah's Ark.

During this time, I was given my first neuropsychological test. I have since had many more, and I hate them, but I didn't know what I was in for the first time. The test, I was told, is usually a daylong process; but because I was experiencing so much fatigue, mine was spread over two days.

The interviewer began, "I'm going to say a word, and I want you to repeat it back to me." That sounded easy enough, and it was.

"Cookie."

"Cookie," I repeated.

"Dog."

"Dog," I said. This went on for a while, and then she gave me two words at a time.

"Red, black."

"Red, black." *Piece of cake*, I thought.

And then she added another word. "Red, black, yellow."

"Red, black . . . " I couldn't remember "yellow." I couldn't remember any of the third words in the lists she gave me. This was true for test after test, and I felt utterly defeated by my inability to remember a simple list of three words.

It was obvious that I wasn't ready yet, but there was no question in my mind that I was going to work as a pastor again, and I was totally focused on that goal. The physicians, nurses, and therapists who work with brain injury survivors are in a tough spot when they have patients like me. They don't want to squelch a person's drive to improve, but they have to be realistic about a patient's limitations.

Some time later, I saw a neuropsychologist who told me I would never be able to work as a minister in a church again. But I didn't believe him. *I'll show him!* I thought. *He just doesn't know what a hard worker I am.* That determination drove me from the beginning and clouded my perception of my deficits.

Several years later, when I was volunteering on a unit at Emory University Hospital where patients are first admitted after sustaining brain injuries, I met a young man who was a tree trimmer. One day, sitting in a wheelchair, he told me with slurred speech that he was going home for the weekend. "I don't think I'll get up in any trees, though," he said.

Thinking he was making a joke, I was about to laugh. But then I realized that he had actually considered it and was utterly serious. Like me with my plan to return to my former work life, he was totally unaware of the gravity of his situation. Such lack of awareness isn't unusual in the early stages of recovery, but during a treatment team meeting, my team told Michael that they were especially concerned about it in my case.

* * *

I learned during this time that some people with brain injuries undergo dramatic personality changes. Reading through my journal, I'm struck by how my worry-wart personality hadn't changed at all. I fretted about losing my job, and I planned—totally unrealistically—to start back part-time in January and be full-time by March. A little personality change might have done me good!

One day my therapist set up a checkbook exercise for me to do and then walked out of the room to work with another patient. I stared at the materials, utterly perplexed. Michael saw that the instructions were not clear, and even he—a former CPA—wasn't sure how to do it.

My mounting frustration grew even more intense. I began to lose trust in my therapists. I'm embarrassed now when I realize how often I thought I was sharper than they were and had a better idea of what was best for me. After hearing me complain every night about my day, Michael suggested that I switch to the other rehab center. I agreed that this was a good idea, and we took the complicated steps required to make the move.

But on February thirteenth, Ash Wednesday, the day before I was to begin the new program, we learned that our insurance company would not approve the change. This contradicted what we had been told, and we were shocked. I still believed that my entire future depended on getting the right therapies in the right place, and this decision threw a big wrench in my plans.

Shaking with rage, I cried and cried that day. *O God, what now?* I prayed in desperation. *I still have so far to go, and I need help . . . Don't you even care about me?*

I had planned to go to the Ash Wednesday service at church that night, but I decided I'd rather stay home. At that moment I felt no hope for the future. I didn't want ashes placed on my forehead. It seemed my whole life was in ashes.

Feeling defeated, Michael and I made an appointment with my physiatrist, the physician who was overseeing my recovery, to ask him what to do. He told us that the most important thing was to keep my brain active, to train new neurons to take over for the ones that had died in the accident. He said that could happen wherever I was. Still disappointed, but relieved, I returned to Meadowbrook for what turned out to be a few more weeks of very good speech and physical therapy.

At this point, I decided that the eye patch I had to wear was so ugly that I needed to decorate it. I became quite the connoisseur of small stickers, having a large collection to fit my moods, my wardrobe, and the seasons: stars, rainbows, smiley faces, and hearts; flowers of all kinds and colors; holiday symbols, including a shamrock, a pumpkin, and a Christmas tree. Not every sticker would do—some totally overwhelmed my small face. As if playing a game, I spent a great deal of time and care each day determining which one I would wear.

Looking back on it now, I see that this was a response to feeling utterly out of control. I couldn't control my environment or the pace of my recovery. I couldn't control my schedule or my fatigue. I certainly couldn't control my future. The one thing I did have control over was the sticker I put on my eye patch each day. And, for a while, that had to be enough.

* * *

The events that followed are hazy, but I do remember that the spring of 1997 was a frustrating and difficult time. I was a stranger to my own life.

I knew I needed to find a vocational therapist. My insurance company told me that more rehab wasn't "medically necessary" and refused to pay for anything except a few more sessions of speech therapy. I was stunned. How could rehab not be "medically necessary" when I still had difficulty completing my sentences and carrying on an intelligent conversation, was unable to read a book or even an article, couldn't drive, could barely write, and had to take naps throughout the day? *Do they even want me to get back to work?* I wondered angrily.

I had even more troubling questions: *Is God ignoring me? Has God taken away my call?*

At one point I wrote in my journal: "I love Michael. I just wish he made more money. Then I could be a 'kept woman.'" I was joking, because the last thing I wanted was to be taken care of by someone else. One of the reasons I had waited so long to marry was that I didn't want to lose my independence. But six months into my marriage, I had lost it utterly and completely.

Mount Vernon Presbyterian Church continued paying my salary through this time—a true gift, especially in light of the fact that I was unable to work. When I learned that I could receive disability payments from both my Presbyterian denomination and Social Security, I decided to leave my position at the church. I felt such a jumble of emotions. I was sad to leave my first placement as a pastor, but I looked forward to finding work that resonated more closely with the call I felt to urban ministry. I was scared to leave the familiar but also excited about new possibilities. I knew the path ahead of me was still long, but I was determined.

On Sunday, May 18, when the elders of the church were gathered for their monthly Session meeting, I officially handed them my resignation letter. My colleague Carol Strickland was sitting next to me. I thought about the treasured notebook she had placed outside my hospital room the day after my accident, where people who came to visit could record their thoughts and good wishes. I pictured the flower pot that the children of the church had painted for me with all their names, and the sweatshirt from the youth group with their names and the words "Someone at Mount Vernon

Loves Me" written in fabric paint. I remembered the generosity of the congregation after my accident. When the pastor prayed, my tears began to fall. Carol reached over and took my hand, squeezing it tightly.

* * *

My plan for the immediate future was to be a full-time volunteer at the Open Door Community. It was where Michael's searching soul eventually had led him, and where we had met. Our relationship had blossomed in the context of the community and its commitments, and we had forged strong friendships there—despite the fact that on one of my earliest visits to Michael when he lived there, a member of the community who didn't recognize my car had it towed from the parking lot late one night! That's when I learned that Michael has a temper.

We moved to an apartment complex closer to the Open Door's home on Ponce de Leon Avenue, a main thoroughfare through downtown Atlanta. Our apartment wasn't as nice as the one we left, but I comforted myself with the thought that this was a temporary move. Just until I returned to a church position.

Michael learned that our income was low enough for me to qualify for funding through the federal Department of Human Resources' Vocational Rehabilitation Services. This covered further physical, cognitive, and vocational therapy at the Shepherd Center in downtown Atlanta, considered one of the nation's top spinal cord and brain injury rehabilitation hospitals. Michael handled the mountain of required phone calls, paper work, applications, details, complications, and hassles in his usual organized fashion.

With compromised vision and a slow reaction time, I still couldn't drive. Getting around when Michael couldn't take me somewhere was complicated, especially when I had to change buses, which was the case for some appointments and whenever I went to the Shepherd Center. I never could remember the bus route numbers. So before every trip, I wrote down the numbers I needed on small pieces of paper, one for each route, and stuck them in my jeans pocket. After a while it occurred to me that I could save and reuse them, and I kept stacks of these tiny slips of paper on a shelf in our office at home. But I often forgot about the papers in my pocket and had to start all over again every time they went through the wash in my jeans and came out illegible.

I had to give myself lots of time to get anywhere. If I missed a bus, I had a thirty-minute wait for the next one. I gained a deep appreciation for all the folks who rely solely on public transportation to get where they need to go, especially in bad weather. I had a few appointments that required taking a MARTA subway train in addition to a city bus. I spent a lot of energy worrying about missing my connection from the train to the bus, and I found it hard to cope with the constant, loud talk at the bus stop. This is when I became really aware of just how much cognitive energy I had lost. I lacked a full set of neurons in my brain to help me manage details and noise, and these trips utterly exhausted me.

Fortunately, it was easier to get to the Open Door. I walked a few blocks to the bus stop and then rode one bus all the way down Briarcliff Road, which left me off a short distance from the community. Early on, my vocational therapist from the Shepherd Center came with me a couple of times to help me figure out how I could perform my responsibilities there.

One of the main ones I was assigned was "phone and door." As you might guess, this job entailed answering the phone . . . and the door. The phone rang frequently with inquiries about volunteering, dropping off donations, and getting information about our services. People from the streets showed up at the door constantly, seeking an aspirin or a pencil, a cough drop or a meal, picking up their mail or getting on the list for a shower or the weekly foot clinic. My job included ushering them back to the clothing room and assisting them as they picked out a shirt or pair of socks, then rushing back to catch the phone.

I learned quickly that "phone and door" was simply more than my brain could handle.

Someone else was assigned to take over the phone while I continued to answer the door. This was better, but responding when the doorbell rang while I was helping a guest inside the house was still challenging. I was also doing other tasks: serving food for the soup kitchen, vacuuming the rugs, cleaning the bathrooms. I found it incredibly difficult to be someone with two master's degrees who couldn't always remember where to find the cleaning supplies and which toilet needed to be cleaned.

After my accident, I experienced severe migraine headaches and tried many preventatives, but those that helped made my fatigue even worse. So every day at 12:30 I had to stumble off to a dark, quiet room for a nap, just to make it through the afternoon. For a while I used a loft room on the second floor, gripping the railing as I went up the steps, always feeling like I was going to faint. After a while overnight guests began staying in that room and I had to find another one—a challenge because I can't think or see straight when I'm really tired. I had to grope my way each day down the stairs to the dark, musty, and often cold basement to find an empty room and bed in which to crash. Often when I got there I crawled under the covers and pulled them up over my head, feeling like a complete failure.

Sometime during those days at the Open Door, I had a thought that seemed more profound to me than anything I had learned in seminary. In one life-shattering moment I had gone from feeling like someone in control—with a clear career path, the privilege of choice, and a measure of power—to being an invisible person on the sidelines, merely trying to cope with each challenge as it came and get through each hour as it unfolded. I wasn't simply feeling called to ministry among the marginalized. I *was* the marginalized.

3

Solidarity

Before my accident, the Open Door Community had helped me to recognize Jesus in people on the margins. I wondered if I could recognize him in me. Could I open myself to see his gospel of good news for those who feel disempowered and invisible in a whole new—and deeply personal—way? I pondered this as I handed out sandwiches and socks.

As time went on, I realized that, although I loved the people and work of the Open Door, the chaotic environment there was simply too much for me. I had to stop volunteering. But the community gave me one particularly memorable and enduring gift. In addition to its work with homeless people, the Open Door ministered to individuals on Georgia's death row.

Exactly six days after I handed in my resignation to the church, I made my first visit to Terry Mincey. I remember feeling a bit nervous whenever I thought about meeting Terry. I had never visited anyone in prison before, let alone someone on death row. What would we talk about? Perhaps we would just sit there staring at each other.

A van from the Open Door made the hour-long trip from Atlanta to Jackson once a month, carrying family members of prisoners and those of us who signed on to make regular visits. On my first visit, as we headed down the long driveway leading to the prison, I was distracted by the two large ponds we passed. So beautiful and calm; so unlike anything I had expected to see on prison grounds.

We pulled into the visitors' parking lot, beneath the guard tower, which was ringed with flowers. Each of us filled out a form on a clipboard, giving information about ourselves and the inmate we were there to see. A guard opened the heavy electronic door to let us in one at a time.

I emptied my pockets—full of change and tissues—and put the contents in a small box along with my driver's license. Then I passed through the first metal detector, hoping the guard wouldn't look at my ankles under my pant cuffs and find what I had hidden there. It was totally harmless—but forbidden under strict prison regulations about "contraband."

Breathing a small sigh of relief when I made it through, I picked up my ID and the change; the tissues were prohibited and had to be surrendered to the guard. I made my way with the other visitors down a very long, dark, underground corridor to a set of stairs. One flight up, I filled out another form and exchanged my license for a round metal badge with a number stamped on it, which I would turn in at the end of my visit to retrieve my ID. I passed through a second metal detector and walked into a holding area as the guard opened the barred electronic door.

I headed straight for the restroom, where I rescued the Chapstick hidden in my sock. I'm a Chapstick addict. My lips have stopped making the oils they're supposed to make, so I use it about three times every hour and am miserable without it. It seemed worth the risk to smuggle it into the prison for the sake of preventing sore and cracked lips.

I walked to the vending machines, filled with candy and cookies and chips, rows of neon-colored sodas, and sandwiches that consisted of gray meat between slices of thin white bread wrapped in plastic. I guessed at what Terry would like and fed the machines from my large cache of quarters.

Then, clutching the stash of snacks, I sat on one of the flimsy plastic chairs and waited for Terry's name to be called. And waited a little longer. Finally, I heard "Mincey." As I watched through the barred door, Terry was escorted into a long, narrow room with wood stools. The guard removed his handcuffs. And then I was ushered in to join him.

Elizabeth and Gladys from the Open Door were also there visiting. They didn't seem at all concerned about being locked up with convicted killers, and I didn't want them to know what I was feeling. *I can do this!* I told myself, glad that I had pushed through my fears to get there. But I shot a glance in the direction of the window at the end of the visiting room, just to make sure the guard was keeping a watch on all that went on.

It didn't take long to discover that Terry and I had plenty to talk about. He was interested in everything. He had a quick, inquisitive mind and spoke very rapidly. He described a Scrabble board he had made out of things on hand in prison—cardboard and paper and candy wrappers—so that he and his best friend, Jack, could play the game regularly. One of his prized possessions was a huge dictionary that he kept in his cell. He flipped through its pages to learn new words, continuing an education that was interrupted during high school.

Terry also loved to work on his family genealogy. One of his cousins helped him with research, and Terry had drawn an elaborate genogram from his notes. To my surprise, he showed me how to write several characters in Japanese. Not allowed paper and pencil in the visiting room, Terry broke off the tab from his Coke can and used it to draw with soda on the counter, wiping away the letters when he was done. He explained that he had a visitor from Japan, a friend of the Open Door, and that he liked to sign his letters in English and Japanese.

Two hours after I arrived, I went back through the barred doors, retrieved my ID, and joined the others in the van. A picnic was going on by the ponds as we drove out, lots of people setting out food and barbecuing on portable grills as ducks and geese swam lazily on the water. I assumed that they were the families of the prison staff. The scene seemed oddly incongruent. I fell asleep wondering how long it had been since Terry Mincey had been on a picnic. I didn't wake up until we reached the Open Door.

* * *

Once a month for four years I smuggled my Chapstick into the prison and visited Terry. I bought him the powdered-sugar donuts he loved so much out of the vending machine. I learned words in Japanese and many new ones in English from his dictionary searches. I heard the pieces of his story and met a few of his friends when they had visitors at the same time.

Those visits were an extraordinary gift to me, but they were not easy. The narrow visiting room had bleak cinderblock walls, uncomfortable stools, and bright, buzzing fluorescent lights. People were packed into it, with children who had come to see their fathers literally bouncing off the walls in the small space—confined and revved up on sugar in its various forms from the vending machine.

Conversations began at a murmur pitch. But as everyone struggled to hear their loved ones, they spoke louder, which caused others to speak even louder, and soon the noise level was a constant, high-pitched cacophony echoing off those bare walls. Terry and I always tried to sit in a corner with my back to the rest of the room, to minimize the stimulation that came at me. But still I had to work very hard to keep my attention and energy focused.

Not having paper and pen was one of the most difficult things. I wanted to remember everything Terry shared with me, but my memory is such that I have a few minutes to write something down before I forget it. By the time I left the prison and headed back to Atlanta, I couldn't remember specifics, although I did try to write a few notes. Aware of my limitations, Terry very kindly often repeated in the letters he wrote to me things he had shared during our visits.

I eventually had to stop riding in the Open Door van. The children visiting their fathers often rode with us. I had always loved children, enjoying their chatter and excitement. Offering the

"Children's Moment" in the Sunday worship service was one of my favorite parts of my church job. But, sadly, after my accident, their loud laughter and boisterous play were problematic for me. I tried muffling the noise with ear plugs, but they didn't help much.

And so I relied on catching rides with friends who were visiting at the prison. On the way there, I always talked for a little while, but then I leaned back, closed my eyes, and spent the rest of the trip doing what I called "resting my brain." After my visits, I slept all the way back to Atlanta and then took a long nap at home. I tried not to schedule anything important in the days following a trip to see Terry, giving myself plenty of time to recover.

My neuropsychologist discouraged these visits because they pushed all my limitations. But I refused to listen to that particular piece of his advice. Those visits were too important to me and worth every ounce of weariness I experienced.

When I first met Terry, the son of a Methodist minister, I thought we needed to talk about God. I was discouraged that we rarely did. I so desperately wanted to be a pastor again, and I thought these visits would help me. Sometimes I planned out questions ahead of time to guide us into faith discussions. But Terry always had a long list of topics he wanted to talk about, and it wasn't easy for me to get in a word, let alone a question. I often asked myself, *What kind of a minister am I if can't even talk with him about God?*

Terry described himself to me as "young and hotheaded" on the late night in April of 1982 when he and two friends committed a robbery at a convenience store in Macon. He shot the cashier, thirty-eight-year-old Paulette Riggs, with his pistol. He was convicted of her murder and sentenced to death in August of that year.

Most of what I know about his case I learned from news reports rather than from Terry himself. His lawyers launched appeals based on the inadequacy of the criminal investigation, evidence withheld at his trial, and eyewitness reports that named one of his accomplices as the killer.

Investigators had removed from Paulette Riggs's back a bullet that was shot from Terry's pistol, but they did not recover the one that was lodged in her skull. A former chief ballistics examiner for the Georgia Bureau of Investigation stated in a sworn affidavit: "It is my expert opinion that an insufficient investigation was conducted concerning the ballistics evidence." He charged the investigators with "improper evidence handling techniques" that resulted in "the loss of crucial evidence." He concluded that, while it was clear that Terry had fired the bullet in Paulette Riggs's back, the presence of only one spent cartridge shell from his pistol by her body indicated that the fatal shot to her head had come from the revolver of one of his accomplices.[1]

Two years before the robbery, Terry had been in a near-fatal motorcycle accident. During his trial, family members testified that he underwent a dramatic personality change, with severe mood swings and impaired memory. But his defense attorney presented to the jury no expert testimony from a medical professional about the possible effects of a head injury on his behavior.

Eight years later, Terry's appeal lawyers discovered notes taken by the prosecutor during a pretrial meeting with the state's psychiatrist, who had evaluated Terry in May 1982. The psychiatrist had concluded that Terry had sustained brain damage in the accident that likely made him "susceptible to irrational behavior." In a 1993 affidavit, a psychologist stated that Terry's head injury would have impaired his judgment and impulse control, establishing his behavior on the night of the crime as "the irrational impulsive actions of a brain damaged individual and not the actions of a cold, calculated, and premeditated murderer."[2]

Terry never denied shooting Paulette Riggs, but he believed that her actual killer testified against him to deflect his own guilt and avoid a death sentence—a tragically common occurrence in capital cases. I don't know exactly what happened on that disastrous night in April 1982, but I do know that Terry would have given anything to undo those fateful few minutes and reverse the terrible suffering of Paulette Riggs's family, and of his own. Who of us wants to be known for the worst thing we've ever done—and

1. Rankin, "Condemned Killer's Guilt."
2. "Amnesty International."

pay for it the rest of our lives? Who wants to live where those who control us believe that we are beyond redemption and deserve to die?

All over a convenience-store cash drawer that held $141.19.

* * *

When I reflect back on my visits with Terry, I think of the parable that opens the eighteenth chapter of the Gospel of Luke. Jesus' hearers were experiencing persecution and hardship and were beginning to give up hope. And so he told them a story about a persistent widow.

The Hebrew Scriptures repeatedly insist on justice for "widows and orphans." Having lost the protection and economic support of a husband, widows were usually poor and subject to exploitation, considered among the most vulnerable members of the society, along with their children. But the judge in the parable obviously didn't care about the mandate for justice, or about what God or people thought of him. He repeatedly refused to respond to the widow's plea.

Her case looked hopeless. But she just kept bothering the judge over and over and over again. "Grant me justice!" she demanded. And eventually even this cold-hearted judge had to give in. He complained that if he didn't, she would wear him out.

When Jesus introduced the story, he told his listeners "not to lose heart." That phrase can also be translated as "don't despair." The antidote to despair is persistence—but also, as the widow shows us, courage.

This parable was Terry's story. He wanted to live. He never gave up. He asked for justice again and again through the court appeals of his lawyers. But in his case, the judge wrote a different ending. In October of 2001, Terry was handed an execution date. He had spent nineteen years—almost half of his forty-one-year life—on death row.

I never could square killing someone with Jesus' command in his Sermon on the Mount to reject "an eye for an eye and a tooth for a tooth" thinking (Matt 5:38). How could the One who told us to love our enemies support state-sanctioned murder? What gives us the right to abandon the hope of transformation for any child of God and limit the reaches of God's grace? As Terry pulled me out of my head and into my heart, my long-standing opposition to the death penalty became more fervent and real.

During the last week of his life, Terry was granted the privilege of extra visiting hours, and I got to meet all the people he had told me about over the years. I learned the day before he was killed that some of his friends liked to talk a lot, interrupting him often when he spoke.

I had come to realize that one of the most important gifts of ministry is the habit of listening. After my accident, the time I needed to process a conversation and pull together a response slowed way down. I was forced to be a more careful listener and a more thoughtful responder. Often I was unable to offer my thoughts about something Terry shared with me until I got back home and put them in a letter.

It finally dawned on me that what Terry had needed more than theological discussions was to share his own experiences and have them heard—and to find out about my life and the world beyond the small cell in which he was confined. I was heartened and grateful that I was able to give him that gift.

As always during an execution in Georgia, vigils were held at the prison. Two areas were roped off near the entrance—one for supporters of the execution and one for those who opposed it—separate and out of view of each other to minimize confrontations.

The Ku Klux Klan was known to show up and cheer when the moment of death was pronounced. I was troubled by that prospect and hoped that they wouldn't. I didn't think I could handle that. It didn't occur to me until later that this wouldn't happen with Terry, because unlike the majority of the people on death row, he wasn't an African American man.

Michael and I, and several folks from the Open Door Community, arrived early. Less than three weeks before, the Georgia Supreme Court had pronounced the electric chair unconstitutional, declaring that electrocution "inflicted needless suffering." Terry's execution was the first in the state to be carried out by lethal injection, and it received a great deal of media attention. As we got close to the prison, I noticed all the news cameras.

I thought I was going to be okay. But when I got out of the car, my eyes filled with tears. Michael and I walked away from the cameras. When I regained my composure, we joined the vigil circle. Those of us who knew Terry shared stories about him. Then we each picked up a candle and lit it.

The constant camera flashes were annoying to me. I felt my frustration growing. A camera flashed in my direction, and I snapped. "Don't take my picture!" I shouted at the photographer as I fell into Michael's arms. Following my outburst, a group of people moved in and stood in front of me to block the cameras. My community.

Inside the prison, I learned later, Terry had finished the last meal of his choosing: fried shrimp, a baked potato, two cans of soda, and a pint of chocolate ice cream. He was in the death chamber strapped to a gurney, his arms outstretched to the walls beside him. The gurney was angled so that he could see the nineteen witnesses in the brightly lit room on the other side of the glass that had come to watch him die. His last words were, "I just want to say to all the people who stood by me, I appreciate it. That's it."

Two guards and a medical technician dressed in a uniform patterned with bright flowers stood next to him. The prison warden read out the execution order as the chaplain squeezed Terry's hand. Terry nodded his head slightly toward the witnesses. Then he looked at the ceiling and closed his eyes as the executioners injected three drugs to sedate him, paralyze his lungs, and stop his heart. He murmured something the witnesses couldn't understand. His breathing weakened and slowed. And then it stopped.

The only sounds were the scratch of reporters' pencils on notepads, the cough of a witness, the sigh of a guard. Two doctors entered the death chamber with the warden. The first took out a stethoscope, put it to Terry's chest, and shook his head "no" to indicate the absence of a heartbeat. Then the second did the same.

Michael and I spent that night in Jackson at New Hope House, a community that offers hospitality to family members and friends of death-row inmates. The next day I was relieved to see that my picture was not in the Jackson newspaper. It was only when I got back to Atlanta that I saw a picture of me, clipped from the *Atlanta Journal-Constitution*, hanging on the bulletin board at the Open Door. Although I had been angry at the photographer at the time, he poignantly caught my sorrow. In spite of my fear about being captured publicly on film at that tragic and vulnerable moment, I believe that God used that picture as a witness to the humanity and dignity of Terry and his brothers on death row.

At 8:06 PM on October 25, 2001, my friend Terry Mincey was killed by the state of Georgia. On the exact same day fifty-six years earlier, Sadako Sasaki died from the effects of the atomic bomb that US forces had unleashed on Hiroshima, Japan. When I discovered her story, I thought of Terry, who loved all things Japanese.

Sadako was two years old when the bomb was dropped a mile from her home in 1945. Ten years later she was diagnosed with leukemia, the result of her exposure to its lethal radiation. According to a Japanese legend, anyone who folds a thousand origami paper cranes will have a wish come true. Twelve-year-old Sadako's wish was to live. Despite her waning strength, she managed to finish about 1,300 cranes, according to her family.

But, as with Terry, her wish to live wasn't granted. A monument stands in Hiroshima in honor of all the children who were killed by the bomb. There is no monument for the men who have been killed by state execution.

When I glimpse the bright royal-blue afghan with lavender stripes that Michael and I have on our bed, I think of the many hours Terry spent crocheting it for us. I remember being amazed when I learned that the men on Georgia's death row taught one another to crochet and share patterns and yarn, making beautiful gifts for their loved ones. I will always cherish that afghan.

But Terry gave me a far greater gift. A brain injury survivor and the victim of a terrible injustice, he showed me how to remain positive and make the most of a challenging situation—at a time when I was struggling mightily to stay hopeful and make sense of my diminished life. And that's a gift I will never forget.

4

Wilderness

After I stopped volunteering at the Open Door Community, I was plagued with one question: What am I going to do with my time? I tried to think of other volunteer opportunities that would prepare me for returning to full-time ministry. Still limited to places I could reach by public transportation, I discovered a hospice for people dying of AIDS not far from our apartment. I was excited about the possibility of spending time there, believing that this would be the perfect place for regaining and sharpening my pastoral skills. I told myself that I wouldn't have been able to volunteer there if I still worked full-time for the church—always trying to put a positive spin on the fact that I had no job.

After the orientation session, filled with hope, I began my visits. I learned rather quickly that the patients at that hospice didn't want to talk. They wanted to sleep. Day after day I went into rooms with residents who were sleeping soundly. The few who were awake made clear to me that they didn't want visitors. I wondered if they felt shame about their stigmatizing disease, or feared that I was an outsider who carried the societal judgment that was often directed toward people with AIDS. But I lacked the cognitive skills to address the dilemma, so I stayed silent and left them in peace. I didn't know what else to do.

Eventually I realized that there was no point in continuing, and I stopped going to the hospice. I was disheartened, feeling unwanted and irrelevant. I was left with nothing but time on my hands. I had been so busy with my rehab and adjusting to so many changes, I hadn't spent much time really thinking about what had happened to me. When I finally did, I sank into a deep depression.

I remembered functioning on six hours of sleep a night, but now I needed at least nine—with a nap or two during the day in addition. I recalled the youth group meetings and Sunday school lessons I had planned, and how easily the words for public prayer had come to me. Now my brain seemed to freeze when I was asked to pray, and I couldn't even begin to organize myself to run a meeting or teach a class—let alone preach a sermon. I struggled just to read a Scripture in church, practicing every word over and over in the days leading up to the Sunday morning when I read aloud for the first time in public after my accident.

And I could not play my violin. I didn't recognize it at the time, but in many ways that was my greatest grief. I had invested only a few years in preparing to be and serving as a minister, but I had been a musician my whole life.

I remembered as if it were yesterday the day in elementary school when I came home and told my parents I wanted to play the violin. They were surprised; no one in my family was interested in classical music. But they let me learn, beginning on a small violin with strips of adhesive tape marking where to place my fingers.

My first solo, played in a school concert when I was in sixth grade, was the rousing "William Tell Overture" (known by most people as the theme song of *The Lone Ranger* TV show). It was a monumental moment for me, and I was a nervous wreck, but it went fine. In Ferndale, Michigan, the small suburb outside Detroit where we lived, I became a leader in my junior high orchestra and for a year in the senior high orchestra as well, aspiring to the honor of concertmaster.

But at the end of my sophomore year, my parents announced that we were moving to Overland Park, Kansas, just outside Kansas City. I was not happy. I had lived in Ferndale my whole life, and I didn't want to move. My parents were understanding and supportive, but my father had accepted a position in his company's home office, so we were going. My violin was my salvation. As an introvert who didn't make friends easily, I was grateful to find my place as a leader in my high school orchestra in Overland Park and in the Kansas City Youth Symphony.

I won a full scholarship to attend the Conservatory of Music at the University of Missouri in Kansas City. Few academic courses were required for a performance degree, so I took the minimum—a choice I now regret—and focused on my music. The violin—and later the viola as well—were my life. I spent many hours—four to six every day—in the small, dark, drab, and windowless practice rooms at the university, hoping to get good enough to be able to make a living as a professional musician someday.

I lived at home the first year and moved onto campus the second, to be more a part of the conservatory community. But, still an introvert who craved solitude, I escaped dorm life and my two roommates as often as possible, adding evening hours to my practice time. Those of us who were performance majors got to know one another, haunting the second-floor practice rooms at all hours, talking in the hall when we took snack breaks. But mostly we practiced.

By then I was playing second violin for one of the more advanced string quartets at the conservatory, honored to be learning from the expertise of the older members. I knew that if I were going to make it into an orchestra, I needed to be good. *Really* good.

During concerts and recitals, we always played our solo pieces by memory. A few times I couldn't remember the notes and had to stop a piece, check the music from the piano part, and go on again. Embarrassed and feeling a sense of failure, I wanted to hide my memory challenges then, as I tried later to hide the more severe ones resulting from my brain injury. As time went on, I learned to make up something if I forgot the notes.

My accompanist, also a student, told me about an apartment available in his complex in a busy shopping and nightlife area of Kansas City, within walking distance of the university. The studio apartment I ended up renting had a bed that pulled out of the wall and a kitchen I couldn't turn around in. But it was mine alone, and I felt all grown up in it.

In a recital my junior year, I played "The Baal Shem Suite: Three Pictures of Hassidic Life," by Ernest Bloch. It's hard for me to explain what happened to me when I played the violin, but perhaps describing this piece will offer a glimpse. It touched my soul in a way few musical pieces had to that point.

The first "picture," or movement, was "Vidui" (Contrition). When I played this somber, meditative piece, I felt like I was pouring out all my questions, doubts, and fears as I was held safely in the arms of God. The second, "Nigun" (Improvisation), soared energetically toward exhilaration and ecstasy, and I felt it mirroring my own uplifted emotions as I floated in God's all-embracing Spirit. The third was "Simchas Torah" (Rejoicing), which the liner notes described as Bloch's "most expansive mood," in which he lavishly poured out his warmth and sense of well-being "as if gathered around a table for a good meal with family and friends." When I played it, I felt God's boundless and never-changing love all around me.

As was always the case, despite having spent endless hours repeating each finger shift over and over again, some of my octaves and double-stops were a little out of tune. I was not the best technician. But I was able to express my emotions through my violin. My spirit and mind went into another world when I played. And I loved going to that place.

* * *

When I had both bachelor and master's degrees in violin performance in hand, I launched my career as a freelance musician in Kansas City, receiving invitations to play at various events through contacts I had developed during my years at the conservatory. I also taught private violin and viola lessons in my parents' living room, grateful for their generous offer of the space until I could afford a studio nearby. I eventually attained the role of assistant concertmaster for the St. Joseph Symphony in St. Joseph, Missouri.

But my most interesting venture by far was as half of an accordion-and-violin duo called Bellows and Bows. We played for a variety of parties and receptions all around Kansas City. Our steady gig was offering classical pieces, waltzes, polkas, and show tunes five days a week during breakfast and lunch at the Hyatt Regency Hotel's coffee shop. I loved seeing the looks on people's faces when they walked in and saw what unusual entertainment awaited them. On Sundays we strolled through the hotel's main restaurant, serenading patrons as they ate their waffles and eggs from the brunch buffet.

I had never been inclined toward a nine-to-five job, and I enjoyed the demanding and unpredictable schedule of a musician. One night I would play my violin as part of Bellows and Bows for a wedding reception, the next morning I'd be in a string quartet with my viola playing a Bach cantata in church, and the following afternoon I'd have a steady stream of children coming for private lessons. Though I enjoyed it all, as time went on I began to realize that I didn't want to spend the rest of my life doing this.

I had been baptized a Methodist as a baby, and church had always been part of my life. During my time at the music conservatory, I served as the choir director for a small, conservative Disciples of Christ church. I had never directed a choir before, but as a music major who could sing, I figured I'd be fine. The church emphasized personal salvation through Jesus Christ, and at that point in my life I felt at home there theologically. After observing a few baptisms in the baptismal pool behind the choir loft, I became convinced that I needed to be baptized again as an adult by immersion. I don't remember much about it, except that the choir was very excited to see their director baptized.

When I left my position with the choir, I became active in the 6,000-member Village Presbyterian Church. I didn't know much about Presbyterian theology, but I was drawn to that particular church. I had often played my violin there when the church hired musicians for orchestras, and I loved the sermons. I taught children's Sunday school, served on the peacemaking committee, and sang in the choir, in addition to continuing as a frequent violin soloist in worship.

As my world expanded, my theology broadened as well. One of the pastors at the church asked me if I had ever considered going to seminary. At first I was stunned, because that thought had never crossed my mind. I had always thought of ministers as "special people," and I didn't think I fit the mold. But he encouraged me to take a few classes at Kansas City's Central Baptist Theological Seminary. I quickly discovered that I loved it.

I decided to continue my theological studies and seek ordination in the Presbyterian Church, which began with needing to have my home church "validate my call." I was nervous in front of such a huge congregation, but I received immediate affirmation. Although it wasn't required, I wanted to switch to a Presbyterian seminary, to fill in the missing pieces in my background. After exploring a few, I settled on Columbia Theological Seminary in Atlanta.

I had not taken classes in the prescribed Presbyterian seminary order, and transferring made me an "out-of-sequence student," so I was required to take courses on several different levels at once. As an older student used to being on my own, I found moving into a dorm again and taking meals in the cafeteria a difficult adjustment. I chafed under the structure and jumped at the chance to move off campus when a professor told me about a former student looking for a roommate in her apartment.

My violin again provided comfort during those days of change and adjustment. I often slipped into the seminary chapel late at night, pouring out both my frustration and joy through my violin. Singing in a local church choir helped as well. After I graduated and began serving as an associate pastor at Mount Vernon, I enjoyed playing in a community orchestra, with people who knew nothing about my life as a minister. Music had always been the center of my life and the way I expressed my emotions, and rehearsals and concerts continued to be respite and delight for me.

* * *

After the car accident, I lost both mental focus and manual dexterity. My musical and pastoral skills were gone, and I didn't know what to do. I had invested so much in my career and future, what was the point of living? *My life is over*, I told myself. I returned to the darkness, spending hours underneath the covers in bed, with Abu snuggled next to me for comfort.

With crisis mode behind us, Michael too had time to think about what had happened. It was inevitable that he would feel guilty about the accident. I know how desperately he wished he could undo those few seconds that changed our life forever.

Couples venturing into a marriage have enough adjustments to make and challenges to work through without such a disaster overtaking them. And even couples who have been together for a long time would have found such a life-shattering experience difficult. Faced with such pressure, many marriages go under.

As Michael watched me languish in bed day after day, he grew understandably angry. He had supported me through the worst, and now that I was home I wasn't responding with the grit and gratitude he expected. Our changed circumstances, both financial and otherwise, derailed his dream of pursuing a graduate degree.

I knew our life would never be "normal." Ever. One day I managed to pull myself out of bed long enough to shout at him, "Why don't you just leave me? I've messed up our life. You'd be better off if you just left!"

Michael didn't hesitate for a beat. "Tamara, I'm not going to leave you. No way would I even consider it."

I was enormously relieved, grateful for his clarity and commitment. Though we hadn't uttered the words "for better or worse" to each other during our wedding ceremony, it was an unspoken understanding between us. Surely, I thought, we had been handed the worst. And Michael was sticking with me. Together, we would figure out this new life.

What finally reached me and pulled me out from under the covers were those words of the prophet Isaiah, still echoing in my brain: "Do not remember the former things, for I am about to do a new thing. I will make a way in the wilderness and rivers in the desert." I felt a small glimmer of hope. I thought, *I can't work as a minister right now, but God is going to make a way for me, I just know it. I just need more time.*

I repeated that Isaiah passage over and over in my mind. What was it that God was going to do for me? I was more than ready for this "new thing." Like the Israelites in exile in Babylon who needed Isaiah's promise, I wanted to believe that God was making a way for me through a difficult and foreign landscape. At the time, I felt lost in the thick of the deepest, darkest, starkest wilderness.

But on my good days I trusted that a way to move forward would be revealed. Sometimes faith is like that: the mind may not believe, but somewhere deep in the heart lies hope.

* * *

Without a clear path, I dragged myself out of bed and started on the way again. I decided to check at the chaplain's office at Wesley Woods, a nearby retirement community, about volunteer possibilities. The thought of walking into a strange office without an appointment and asking if help was needed was a little overwhelming, but I was desperate. Michael drove me there and waited in the car while I went inside to see if I could find someone to speak with.

By providence, as we Presbyterians like to say, I ran right into Woody Spackman, the head of the chaplaincy department. He told me that a full-time Clinical Pastoral Education (CPE) program affiliated with the Emory Healthcare System met at the office, which was usually a bustle of activity. But it was between sessions, and on that afternoon the office was unusually quiet. Woody dropped what he was doing and invited me in.

I explained that I was a Presbyterian minister looking for a place to volunteer. I mentioned my accident and told him that I had a "head injury." I had always prided myself on my intellectual ability, and I felt that using the term "brain injury" would sound as though I couldn't think anymore. And I certainly didn't use the word "disability." It was a very negative term to me then, and I thought that only people who couldn't work or participate in society had disabilities. That certainly wasn't me.

Woody listened. He gave me a short tour of the community's campus. And then he graciously invited me to join the staff as its first volunteer chaplain. As at the hospice, I took the volunteer training, but I didn't like being considered a volunteer. In fact, when the staff members at Wesley Woods wanted to give me the Volunteer of the Year award after my second year, I turned down the honor and told them to pick someone else. (That was a first for them.)

A bus passed right by our apartment and went directly to the retirement community, so my plan worked out well. I wore tennis shoes until I got there, then pulled my dress shoes out of my bag and put them on. I wanted to be professional in every way. Like a lot of people, I saw my work as my identity, and this was now my job—at least until I could enter the call process again.

Each chaplain had an area of the facility for which they were responsible. My first assignment was in Budd Terrace, a building with seven floors. I had a weak sense of direction before my accident, and afterward my spatial disorientation became severe. I frequently walked down a hallway and entered a resident's room, then forgot which way to turn when I left. So I decided to visit each room on one side of the hallway, going in the same direction until I finished, and then start down the other side. It was a great plan, but sometimes a resident hailed me for a conversation from the far end of the hallway, or called me into a room, and then it was easy for me to get disoriented again and forget where to go next.

My neuropsychologist broke down memory issues into three parts: getting information into one's brain, storing it, and retrieving it. I'm able to get information into my brain and hold it, but retrieving it is difficult, which has been confirmed again and again in my neuropsychological evaluations. In order to retrieve information, I need to write it down. This is one of many "compensatory strategies" that those of us with brain injuries use to make up for things our brains are no longer able to do. It's easy to do in one place, but it was challenging when I was visiting several rooms on one floor at Budd Terrace.

My rehabilitation therapist encouraged me to keep a notebook with notes about each resident so I wouldn't get them mixed up. I was embarrassed, because none of the other chaplains did this. But I quickly found that I could not remember what each resident said if I didn't write it down. First I tried a three-by-five-inch notebook that I could hide in my pocket so the residents wouldn't see it. But it was too small to be useful, so I experimented with a few larger ones. I finally settled on a black cover that held a legal notepad, deciding it didn't look overly conspicuous.

At home after each visit, I transferred my notes onto separate papers, which I kept in a spiral-bound notebook. Although I volunteered only a few hours each week, this was a lot of work for me. I have never recovered my cursive writing ability, and printing by pen with the special foam-rubber grip I have to use is extremely time-consuming. Looking back on it now, I recognize that I was trying to rebuild some of the damaged neuropathways of my brain by taking short notes and then filling them out later.

When I was a student at Central Theological Seminary in Kansas City, I had completed a basic unit of Clinical Pastoral Education. I loved it and wanted to do more. The CPE program that included Wesley Woods as a site was an extended unit spread over an entire year, which seemed doable to me. I applied. I was not accepted. Another big disappointment. But deep inside, I think I knew it was for the best. I wasn't ready yet. Instead, Woody offered to personally supervise me in my volunteer visits. He had such wisdom and knowledge about older people, and I was honored to work with him.

I felt privileged to be able to visit the residents, because I knew they were near the end of their lives and I loved hearing their stories. I particularly enjoyed visiting Frances Pauley, who had worked with other churchwomen in the late 1930s and '40s to establish public health clinics in DeKalb County, Georgia. She was known for her story-telling ability, and once a year she related true tales from her long involvement in social justice movements as the guest speaker at the Open Door Community, which is where I had first met her.

Frances had a bird feeder attached to her window and happily spent hours watching the birds that gathered there. She reflected to me once that it surprised her that after all her years of working for racial equality, affordable health care, and economic justice, she was fascinated by these little creatures that came to visit. She reminded me that, while it is important to work for social change, it is just as important to stop and see what God has given us, sometimes right outside our window.

* * *

The first time I helped to lead a devotional service on one of the Alzheimer's units in The Tower at Wesley Woods, I looked out at the sea of people and felt overwhelmed. About forty residents sat in their wheelchairs lined up in rows, and a few more were in folding chairs up front. Their individual rooms lined the hallways on both sides of the large room where I stood, where meals were also served and other group activities took place.

All the faces blurred together. At that stage in my recovery, too much cognitive energy would have been required for me to focus and distinguish them. I gazed out blankly. When the service was over, I felt utterly drained.

My forty-five-minute midday naps were still non-negotiable. I struggled with this, being the only person I knew that still had to do this so long after sustaining a brain injury. I always kept ear plugs in my purse in case I needed to disappear and take a nap. I was sensitive to any sort of stimulation when I was trying to sleep—even the ticking of a clock.

I came to enjoy leading the weekly devotional services on the assisted-living floor, which only a few people attended. I used a table to mark off a place in the lobby, covered it with a cloth and lit a candle on it, creating an intimate space for prayer, sharing stories, and reading Scripture together.

I remember the moment when it occurred to me that I was regaining cognitive and physical function just as the residents at Wesley Woods were losing theirs. Though I had separated the disease of Alzheimer's from my brain injury, we had met on common ground, ultimately going different directions but walking alongside one another for a time. When I was unable to verbalize deeply held thoughts and feelings, which was often, I reminded myself that each person there also had unexpressed feelings. And this knowledge freed me to connect with them on a level deeper than words.

I learned that the best way to lead a devotional service for people with Alzheimer's was to repeat the same songs over and over. They loved "This Little Light of Mine" and "Amazing Grace." "If You're Happy and You Know It" got some up on their feet, clapping and stomping. Others nodded and waved as they sat in their wheelchairs. I often forgot that I even had a brain injury as I sang the songs again and again, clapping and swaying to the music along with them.

Over time, individuals emerged out of the sea of faces. One of my favorites was an African American man I knew only as Deacon, which was the role he had played in his church for many years and the name he wanted his friends to use. We shared a love of singing. Deacon never missed a service, and I came to rely on his resonant bass voice in the front row. He often added harmony—and a few heartfelt "Amens."

Deacon's eyes literally lit up when he sang. Together, he and I always led our favorite song. "Oh, when the saints . . . " I would sing out to the group.

"Oh, when the saints . . . " boomed Deacon's deep voice in response, inviting the others to join him.

"Go marching in . . . " I continued.

"Go marching in . . . " echoed Deacon, his face glowing in the light of God's Spirit.

We always ended together: "Oh, Lord, I want to be in that number, when the saints go marching in."

5

Hope

During the time that I was working at Wesley Woods, I began meeting with Paula Buford, a Baptist pastor in Atlanta who had also sustained a brain injury. Our conversations were life-changing for me. She listened. She offered the comfort that came from knowing that I wasn't alone in my struggles to cope with particular challenges and changes. And she introduced me to Nancy Eiesland's book *The Disabled God*, which we discussed sometimes when we were together.

Eiesland's book, with the subtitle *Toward a Liberatory Theology of Disability*, astonished me. I had been introduced and drawn to liberation theology in seminary. I had begun to understand Jesus as a person of color, a Jew in an occupied country, a homeless and penniless wanderer who challenged injustice on behalf of those who were hurting and poor and oppressed.

Nancy Eiesland showed me that, entirely consistent with Jesus' marginalized life, at death his body was pierced and broken. It was disabled.

I received from her a beautiful reminder to hold and cherish: When we participate in the Eucharist, grace comes to us through a broken body. "This is my body, broken for you . . ." Knowing this truth, how could I try to hide what was true about my body? How could I consider myself any less sacred or whole than people with "normal" bodies and brains?

I didn't have to look far to discover the source of my prejudice and shame about disability. The lessons I had grown up with had seeped into my pores.

"Who sinned, this man or his parents, that he was born blind?" asked the disciples of Jesus, in a story that opens the ninth chapter of the Gospel of John (John 9:2). Disability and disease have long been equated with sin. The purity codes reminded our ancestors in the faith: "One who is blind or lame, or one who has a mutilated face or a limb too long, or one who has a broken foot or a broken hand, or a hunchback, or a dwarf, or a man with a blemish in his eyes or an itching disease of scabs or crushed testicles shall not come near the altar of God, or make an offering, or serve as a priest of the people" (Lev 21:18–20). And of course women were disqualified for lacking altogether the necessary body parts to carry out sacred duties or approach holy places.

Among the biblical prophets, healing and restoration of physical wholeness were equated with redemption and spiritual strength. My favorite, Isaiah, proclaimed this post-exilic vision of restoration for God's people in a sister passage to the one that had brought me such hope throughout my rehabilitation:

> Then the eyes of the blind shall be opened,
>   and the ears of the deaf unstopped;
> then the lame shall leap like a deer,
>   and the tongue of the speechless sing for joy
> (Isa 35:5–6a).

Jesus quoted the prophet in his inaugural sermon in his hometown of Nazareth. Handed a scroll of Isaiah in the synagogue, Jesus turned to a passage and read it as a way of announcing the call that God's Spirit had put upon him "to bring good news to the poor . . . to proclaim release to the captives and recovery of sight to the blind" (Luke 4:18). And, clearly, healing was a major focus of Jesus' ministry.

I had always been fascinated by the biblical story of the man with paralysis, whose persistent and resourceful friends removed the roof above Jesus and lowered him on his mat into the room when the crowd outside made it impossible for them to enter by the usual route. But Nancy Eiesland pointed out that there are a few issues with the portrayal of this healing as a story about "a crippled sinner and his heroic helpers."[1]

The Mark version states, "When Jesus saw their faith, he said to the paralytic, 'Son, your sins are forgiven'" (Mark 2:5). The story seems to reinforce the idea that sin was responsible for the man's condition—and gives credit to the faith of his friends for saving him. The man with paralysis is therefore not only a charity case, helpless without his friends, but also apparently at fault for his own suffering. The John version ends with Jesus commanding, "Do not sin any more, so that nothing worse happens to you" (John 5:14).

The woman with a twelve-year hemorrhage at least took responsibility for her own well-being, boldly reaching out to touch Jesus' cloak. Jesus healed her and declared, "Daughter, your faith has made you well" (Mark 5:34). It's a beautiful and moving story. But, along with the other healing narratives, many Christians interpret it to mean that if we just have enough faith, we can be cured. Instantly, if we're really good.

I was well aware that I couldn't be "cured."

The accident robbed me of some capacities that I will never get back. As difficult as it was, and often still is, to accept this truth, it was even harder living with the pressure that I was somehow to blame—because I wasn't good enough, or my faith wasn't strong enough. This injustice has been foisted on all sorts of vulnerable people, compounding suffering with shame.

* * *

When the disciples asked Jesus whose sin was to blame for the man's blindness in the John 9 story, he answered, "Neither this man nor his parents sinned; he was born blind so that God's works might be revealed in him" (John 9:3). When I read this, I thought,

---

1. Eiesland, *The Disabled God*, 71.

So I guess those of us with disabilities have to suffer so the rest of you can know about the power of God!

Eiesland addressed this as well. If we aren't fallen sinners, then we're spiritual superheroes. She wrote that the idea of "virtuous suffering," with its implication that God imposes sickness and disability on some particularly strong souls as a form of divine testing to inspire everyone else, is as pervasive and problematic as the Christian paternalism that would reduce us to helpless objects of pity. She saw both as damaging and dangerous. Those of us with disabilities are neither specially damned nor specially blessed.

Accepting my limitations while living into my full potential has been a difficult dance, one with intricate steps I am still learning. I have found it helpful when the people around me understand the special effort it takes to live with a brain injury. But I don't want my life to be an inspiring Hallmark story.

Ironically to me now, I preached my first sermon as a theological student—on March 6, 1990, in the chapel at Central Baptist Theological Seminary in Kansas City—in the first-person voice of a simple, first-century fisherman's wife who suffered pain and isolation as a result of leprosy. My text was Jesus' feeding miracle (Mark 6:30–42). I offered her perspective as a woman hungry for healing and connection, who joined the throng that flocked around Jesus' boat as he arrived on the Sea of Galilee. I assigned to her feelings that would have reflected the understandings of her time and culture: "The priest said I was unclean . . . I know what I felt. Rejected. Separated. Alone. A sinner."

I ended my sermon with this woman receiving bread blessed by Jesus but turning away in fear and shame from the opportunity to be healed: "When it came time to leave, I dallied. I wanted to meet the man in the boat. I thought maybe he could heal me. I wanted my life back. I walked up to him after everyone but his closest followers had gone. I walked up to him slowly. But then I saw his followers. I saw them and I could walk no farther. The man in the boat looked at me. I turned around and walked away."

When Nancy Eiesland wrote *The Disabled God* in 1994, forty-three million people in the United States—one in six—had a disability. I barely noticed. People who used wheelchairs, assistive animals, or sign language were always "other" to me. Until I became part of their community. After my accident, with the help of Eiesland's book, I began to pay attention.

When Jesus appeared to his disciples after his crucifixion, they were "startled and terrified, and thought that they were seeing a ghost" (Luke 24:37). He invited them to look at his hands and feet, to touch his flesh. His friends recognized the resurrected Jesus by his wounds—"revealed as the Disabled God," in the words of Eiesland.[2] She spoke of disability as compatible with full personhood, inviting those of us with disabilities to see ourselves as reflecting the image of God, not in spite of our impairments, but through them.

My mind was reeling and my heart racing as I read those words. Maybe my life wasn't over after all. Perhaps I wasn't "damaged goods," but someone with a voice and something to say. I felt flooded with an even more intense hope, glimpsing and beginning to grasp a new way to be in the world.

Still, not a day went by that I didn't long to have my old life back.

* * *

Through the Shepherd Center, I learned to drive again, which gave me a renewed sense of independence and opportunity. I began attending Oakhurst Presbyterian, a progressive, racially mixed church very involved in social justice activities. Michael joined me occasionally, but he preferred the quiet of the Quaker meeting, where he attended regularly. I loved Oakhurst's services, led by Nibs Stroup, though they were often very long and I still needed my daily 12:30 nap. So I had to skip the fellowship time after church every week, which was probably just as well—the setting was too boisterous and noisy for me to be able to meet and talk with people easily.

2. Ibid., 94.

I didn't want to risk driving the ten miles home when I was overly tired, but finding a place to nap at Oakhurst after church was even more challenging than locating one at the Open Door. In the beginning I rested on a couch in a quiet room where Jill Ulrici, a Presbyterian minister and Reiki therapist, worked. That was fine until winter, when the heat was shut off there, making it too uncomfortable. Two other rooms had couches, but meetings were sometimes held after church in one, and when I was in the other the sounds of the meeting seeped through my ear plugs.

Once a month, Jill led a small and intimate healing service, in which she offered a devotional and then invited those of us who attended to request prayers. The group would surround an individual, lay hands on him or her, and pray. Though hope always attended our prayers, we were not attempting to "cure" anybody. We were seeking the comfort, support, acceptance, and peace that are part of healing rather than cure.

I found it to be a deeply meaningful and encouraging time. But because the services were in the evening and I didn't drive well after dark, I attended regularly only after Michael and I bought a house closer to the church in September 2001. I was able to navigate side streets with a few bright streetlights to get there, and I was very grateful.

When Jill left to take a pastoral position at another church, I was asked to lead the group. I enjoyed doing it, but it pushed my brain's executive functions to the limit. Though it was a simple service, in order to keep things straight I had to write down what I was going to say—even the shortest statements—or I would forget.

Since becoming a Presbyterian, I had always been active in meetings of the presbytery, as well as at whatever church I was attending. And Presbyterians have lots of meetings! I decided to serve on Oakhurst's Outreach Committee and Health Ministry Committee.

Though it was almost six years after my accident, I didn't truly understand how difficult meetings are for people with brain injuries. A meeting involves aspects of cognition that I had always taken for granted. I had to understand and be able to respond to what was being said over a sustained period of time, but my ability to pay attention had been injured. Sometimes we met in an open space, with people walking by and talking, which was especially distracting. I had to make myself focus and practice what's called "selective attention."

When someone made a comment, it took me longer than others to process the information. Often by the time I had a response, the conversation had already shifted to another subject. It was particularly challenging when meetings wandered off topic, with folks bringing up subjects other than the original one. It's hard for me to shift my attention back and forth without getting confused. Spending so much cognitive energy focusing in the meetings wore me out completely.

During rehab I had taken a class on brain function in which these challenges were covered, but I hadn't internalized the information. And I knew that in order to improve, I had to push myself to retrain my brain's neurons. Looking back, I realize that I didn't have a real understanding of what I was up against. After a meeting, I often would have to spend a day or two sleeping to recover.

But I kept rising to the challenges and returning. I also decided to serve on the Health Ministry Committee of the Presbytery of Greater Atlanta. And when I began to feel that I wasn't contributing enough, I offered to take the minutes. I don't know what I was thinking. It was difficult for me to both listen and take notes, so I had to tape the meetings and then listen to them all over again as I sat at the transcribing machine at home. The burden of this began to feel enormous.

Around this time I came to accept that I have a disability. I took to heart Nancy Eiesland's clear word that disability is not something about which I need to feel ashamed. I thought back to my ignorance about disabilities when I was serving a church, and I felt called to work in some way in this area, to help enlighten other pastors.

I formed a subcommittee of the presbytery's Health Ministry Committee focused on disabilities and the church. I knew I didn't have the skills to lead it alone, so I asked Peter Marshall, who attended Mount Vernon Presbyterian Church, to be co-moderator with me. Organizing wasn't the strength of either of us, but he was very knowledgeable and active in the disability field, and we worked hard and persevered.

The highlight of our work was pulling together a Disability Awareness and Training Workshop, which was led by Mark Crenshaw, then the director of the Interfaith Disabilities Network. We held it before a presbytery meeting, which brought together all ordained Presbyterian pastors as well as representatives from each Presbyterian church in the Greater Atlanta area. So many people attended our workshop that we had to bring in extra chairs. It was a brief, bright success in a long season of frustration for me.

But I, too, was a certified success, according to the Shepherd Center. My final evaluation declared that I was rehabilitated enough to "go back to being a homemaker." I have enormous respect for people who feel called to nurture families and maintain homes, but that has never been my calling. The state of my house attests to that. Nonetheless, I had to accept that my rehabilitation was at an end. I pondered my limited possibilities.

I decided to apply again for the Clinical Pastoral Education program, and this time I was accepted. Normally a CPE intern must do "on-calls," staying at work overnight and responding to any needs that come up. Because I was not able to do these, I did more visits during the day. My favorite area was the brain injury unit at the Emory Rehabilitation Center, which gave me a new plan for my future. I thought that having a chaplain with a brain injury would be a great benefit to the patients and their families.

But being on the unit was a huge challenge. The bustle and constant voices of doctors, nurses, CNAs, and technicians in the halls overwhelmed me. Sometimes in the hours just after an accident had happened, an entire family was in a patient's room talking, trying to make sense of an event that had changed everything. I know now that it's important to minimize noise, especially right after an accident, but I didn't have a clear enough understanding then to speak up on behalf of the patients.

Trying to manage the cognitive overload tired me greatly and ultimately became unbearable. At the beginning of the year, I had high hopes for my future. By the end, I realized that being a chaplain in such an environment wasn't going to be a possibility.

What now?

6

Broken

In the summer of 2003, Michael and I took a camping trip to the mountains near Asheville, North Carolina. I had been to several Presbyterian youth conferences at Montreat, a retreat center not far from Asheville, and I knew how beautiful the area is. The trip was a good break for us. Camping was a new experience for me, and I enjoyed it. We brought Abu and spent a week sleeping in our tent, cooking meals on a camp stove, reading and talking by the French Broad River. Each morning I plugged my single-cup coffee pot into the outlet in the public bathroom to make my freshly ground coffee. I can do rugged, but not instant coffee!

Michael was working as the team leader of a psychosocial rehabilitation program at the time and was ready for a change. He came across a Mental Health Association flyer with an ad announcing a new program, seeking someone to serve on a team in Asheville that would provide counseling for people who live on the streets. Michael had enjoyed such work at the Open Door and decided to reply to the ad.

We didn't have a cellphone then, so he used his last bit of change to call from the camp's pay phone. He was invited to go for an interview the next day. He explained that he had only his camping clothes with him, and the person on the other end of the phone didn't seem to mind. So while I waited in the car, Michael showed up for his interview in his cutoff shorts and faded T-shirt. Apparently it went well. He had a follow-up interview by phone after we returned home and then was hired to join the team.

I too was ready for a change. My limitations were beginning to get to me at Wesley Woods. The chaplains there were very busy, as chaplains in any organization are. I watched as they attended weekly staff meetings and other gatherings across the campus. They visited residents, led services, talked with medical personnel, and wrote reports with ease, as far as I could tell. But I lacked the mental flexibility to juggle so many responsibilities. I could do only one thing at a time, and I was beginning to feel bored.

As I left, I graciously accepted the honor when the Wesley Woods staff gave me a Special Service Award for my years of work, feeling regret that I had turned down the Volunteer of the Year honor earlier. I was beginning to understand that being "only a volunteer" was going to have to be okay for me.

* * *

Moving to Asheville felt like a good change. But Atlanta had been home for twelve years, and leaving was harder than I had imagined. Most people have difficulty in a new environment, but for someone with a brain injury who has major spatial orientation issues, change is particularly stressful. I had to start all over to learn and remember how to get places, carefully keeping a folder with directions to just about everywhere.

Michael and I were living in a small apartment, hoping that our house in Atlanta would sell soon. We had left some of our belongings there and had to put others into a storage unit in Asheville, which happened to be located by the Swannanoa River. Soon after we moved, a torrential rain swept through on the tail of a massive hurricane, causing the river to overflow and flood our unit, a calamity that had never occurred to us as a possibility. We got the news from Michael's mother in Indiana, who was the contact person we had listed when we rented the space, before we had a phone.

We began digging through our mud-soaked belongings to determine what we could salvage. The greatest loss was my library; most of the books I owned had been in the storage unit. The added stress made my usual cognitive challenges even worse. I got into a state that's difficult to describe. When it happens, I'm unable to focus, my eyes become clouded, and things blur together; I become weak and my balance is compromised. To others I may look entirely normal, but Michael can easily tell when it's happening. He took me back to our apartment so that I could "rest my brain" while he continued the arduous work of sorting through our damaged possessions. And I compounded my stress by adding feelings of inadequacy and guilt for not being able to help.

In Asheville my physician became concerned that my heart rate was elevated, which she believed was caused by the medication I was taking to prevent migraine headaches. She strongly recommended that I go off the medication. I knew she was right, but my headaches immediately increased. I got some relief through acupuncture, massage, and essential oils—treatments Asheville has in abundance—but still the headaches plagued me from time to time. On the up side, once I stopped taking the pills, for the first time in a dozen years I no longer needed a daily mid-day nap.

I had learned about Circle of Mercy—an ecumenical congregation in Asheville aligned with the United Church of Christ and the Alliance of Baptists—from one of the founding co-pastors, Joyce Hollyday, whom I had met when she was a seminary student at Emory and a volunteer at the Open Door. I was especially drawn to the congregation's mission statement: "We are followers of Jesus who believe that doing justice and loving mercy are intimately tied to walking humbly with God. Our mission is to nurture spiritual formation in ways that support prophetic and redemptive work in the world." I began attending regularly.

I also wanted to stay connected to the Presbyterian Church. Because Circle of Mercy meets on Sunday evenings, I was able to go to the 8:30 AM service at Grace Covenant Presbyterian Church, an outreach-oriented congregation that serves Asheville and the surrounding area in a variety of ways.

Being part of these faith communities has been wonderful for me, but it has also highlighted one of my most difficult and embarrassing limitations. I sometimes get introduced to someone and immediately forget their name. Or, worse, I forget the names of people I've known for a long time or that I see every week.

At Grace Covenant one Sunday morning, I saw someone I needed to speak with walking on the other side of the church narthex. I had talked with him many times, but I couldn't pull up his name. I remember thinking, *Oh, man, he's going to get away, and he's so close; I have to get his attention somehow.* I decided to yell for him. I knew a simple "Hey you!" would have seemed rude and unprofessional. I called out, "Hey you, walking by the library!" I realize in retrospect that my addition wasn't much of an improvement, but it was the best I could come up with in the moment.

He approached me. It's always challenging to know how to react when I'm forced face-to-face with my weakness. Should I make light of it, try to laugh it off? Or will that offend the other person and make a bad situation worse? Should I explain that people with brain injuries often have trouble remembering names? Or will that be perceived as too much information? I mumbled apologetically, "I'm sorry, I'm not good with names."

He responded immediately, "Oh, don't worry about it. I'm not either."

It's a common response, one that I know is intended to be supportive and make me feel more comfortable. But such simplistic efforts at empathy just make me feel discounted and misunderstood. He had no idea what I was up against. Seething inside, I was—silently, of course—yelling at him for his ignorance. But being a "proper" person who isn't in the habit of expressing my anger, I just smiled and nodded.

* * *

Apart from church, I didn't have much social contact. I enjoyed taking walks with Abu near our apartment on a small stretch of the gorgeous Mountains-to-Sea Trail, which spans the length of

North Carolina. But—despite how challenging it often was for me—I craved more human interaction. I decided I wanted to work again with people who have Alzheimer's disease and discovered a place a twenty-minute drive from our apartment called the Black Mountain Neuro-Medical Treatment Center. The center specializes in care for individuals who, because of combative or assaultive behaviors, aren't able to find placements in nursing homes. I volunteered there weekly for two years, never witnessing any violent behavior or feeling unsafe.

But I still had a lot of time on my hands and a desire to find other meaningful work to do. Ellen Frost, the owner of Bed and Biscuit, a boarding and daycare facility for dogs, regularly brought therapy dogs to the center. I saw how much the dogs lifted the spirits of the residents there, as they had at Wesley Woods, and how good Ellen was with them. I sometimes "borrowed" the dog of the center's executive director to work alongside Ellen.

I commented to her one day that I thought I would really enjoy training a therapy dog. Abu was getting up in age, and I knew she was too old to learn new tricks. So I was glad when Ellen responded, "I think I have the perfect dog for you."

She had been boarding Sparky, who prior to arriving at Bed and Biscuit had been determined by a local rescue organization to be part German shepherd and part Chihuahua. Unable to picture how *that* could have happened, I believe Sparky's parentage is probably something quite different—though he does indeed look like a toy version of a German shepherd. The family that had adopted him as a puppy was expecting the real thing, and when he stopped growing at twenty pounds, they dumped him in a shelter.

When I visited Sparky the first time, he greeted me with his whole back end shaking in glee and his tail wagging excitedly. He looked so joyful, I couldn't help smiling. He is a compact bundle of energy and an aptly named handful that Michael and I knew would be challenging. But we saw in him playful sparks of passion, persistence, and curiosity—the traits that Ellen also recognized. After taking him on a test walk with Abu, who sadly passed away soon after that, we decided to adopt him so that I could begin his training.

We thought we could overlook the fact that by eight months old Sparky had been kicked out of three family homes and a kennel run by the director of the Animal Compassion Network. But it didn't take long for us to wonder if he was a good match for us. Michael and I are introverts who like to walk and read and have quiet conversations. Sparky likes to run and wrestle and bark. When we showed up at a puppy obedience class, he barked wildly and non-stop at the other dogs.

And, unfortunately, there was this pesky biting problem, which hadn't presented itself when Sparky was in Ellen's care. We hired a private trainer for an evaluation session. She surmised that Sparky probably had been taken from his mother too early and never learned to bite softly. She told me that I could either work very, very hard with him, or just try to "manage the problem."

Clearly smart, Sparky learned commands quickly, and I focused intently on his training for a while, taking him through exercises over and over. It was exhausting and brought no visible change in his behavior. I decided then that management was realistic.

Then one day Sparky bit me on the hand, making a wound so deep that Michael had to take me to the urgent care center to get it treated and bandaged. The doctor told us that he was required to report the bite to Animal Control, and Sparky had to be quarantined in our house for a week. We weren't supposed to take him for walks or let him run, and that only made him more crazily frenetic.

Michael and I have learned to manage Sparky's imperfections, and he has become a quite loveable member of our household. Rather than being a bad match, we now consider him a much-needed spark of energy amid the dutifulness and routine of our life. But long before he bit Michael and we suffered through a second quarantine, it was more than obvious that he was not cut out to be a therapy dog. And, always anxious to be the center of attention, he would never have tolerated us bringing another dog into the family and making it the focus of therapy-dog training.

I found it hard to know whether to laugh or cry.

* * *

I decided to turn my interest in a different direction. The next thing that caught my attention was a class on clowning offered by Asheville Health Adventures. I'm not entirely sure why. Maybe unconsciously I was anxious to escape from my own life and take on a different identity.

I did an internet search and found quite a few websites about clowning, including information about the Caring Clown movement, which is committed to cheering up folks in medical settings. I was particularly interested in going into nursing homes. Since I still wasn't driving well at night, I rode a bus into downtown Asheville for the evening classes.

I don't remember much about them, except for feeling a little out of place, since I'm not an outgoing person and most of the other participants were. We spent a lot of time talking about our clown characters and how to put on make-up. When it came time for me to choose a character, I decided to be Raindrop, since I've always been drawn to water. I got a curly red wig and a polka-dot shirt from a costume store and had two pairs of pants with elastic at the ankles made for me. I bought some boldly striped socks and found two pairs of tennis shoes on sale, one bright green and the other white with blue stars. I followed a classmate's suggestion and added a colorful umbrella to my costume.

I tend to be serious all the time, and being Raindrop gave me permission to act foolish. I could forget someone's name, drop things, or trip, and it was okay. I didn't have to worry about making a fool of myself because I was supposed to be a fool. When I got lost trying to find the park where I was supposed to mingle with other clowns for an event, I wasn't even embarrassed when I had to go into a gas station in my costume and classic bright-red fake nose to ask for directions. Raindrop freed up a childlike part of my personality.

But this too had its down side. I remember well the day that I was part of a skit in the clown troupe's annual show for family members, friends, and guests. I had been asked to bring my violin and play a simple song, which I thought by then I could do. I had practiced hard at home. At the event I couldn't find a music stand, so I put my music on a table and stood by it.

When the moment came for me to play, despite all my practice and concentration, I knew I sounded like a beginner, barely able to scratch out the simplest of tunes. I longed to be able to pour my emotions freely into my violin again, to lose myself in the sheer joy of playing. I had fallen so far, and the pain in the pit of my stomach felt almost unbearable—a sharp response to a wound that I knew would never disappear. It was clear that Raindrop was not someone I could hide behind.

I don't remember making a conscious decision to stop clowning, but I think it had partly to do with the fact that it took me over an hour to put on my make-up, which was longer than some of my visits. I was often already exhausted before I got to where I was going. The other clowns in the troupe lost interest in visiting nursing homes, and I got tired of going alone. After we lost our leader, the energy in the troupe dissipated, and it eventually disbanded after I left.

* * *

Adding to our stress, when Michael and I learned we had a potential buyer for our house in Atlanta, we returned to discover that someone had broken in and stolen some treasured paintings and furnishings we had left behind. On top of that, after the house finally sold, the movers we had hired to bring out what was left of our possessions never showed up. We had to scramble to find friends to help us.

I craved some peace and stability. Michael and I bought a home with a sunny front yard off a busy street in booming West

Asheville, where we still live. Knowing people who find gardening calming and therapeutic, I thought maybe I could, too. I planted some vegetables among black-eyed Susans and irises, phlox and foxglove, lamb's ear and lavender. A neighbor contributed a sprawling prickly pear cactus. By mid-summer I was enjoying a proud display of bright flowers and harvesting yellow squash and cherry tomatoes.

And then the Bermuda grass attacked. The ubiquitous grey-green stalks of the invasive weed—also known as "devil's grass"—threatened to take over every inch of my garden, choking out the other plants. As soon as I pulled out a clump, it spread through its underground stealth root network and pushed up somewhere else.

I developed osteoarthritis, which brought recurring pain in my right hand. Two surgeries—one to add cartilage where bone was rubbing against bone, and the other a total replacement of my thumb joint—did not correct it. Weeding became a virtually impossible task. Michael and I hired someone to come and dig up the Bermuda grass. Within a month, it was all back.

Okay, if not gardening, maybe art. Michael is an award-winning carver of birds, the creator of many lifelike and awe-inspiring painted wood statues. We already had an art room in our home, and I had enjoyed dabbling in polymer clay at one point. I thought maybe I could be an artist, too.

So I dug out my clay, my roller and blade, and my hand-cranked pasta machine—purchased on an artist's advice for pressing out the clay into strips. When I found the cranking too difficult for my hand, I invested in a motorized version. I made jewelry, mostly earrings. Some are actually quite beautiful. But I grew impatient with it. As with my violin playing, I discovered that I was more interested in expression than technique. I didn't really want to be a jewelry artist.

I joined the choir at Grace Covenant, which suited my artistic expression better. I also began visiting homebound elders in the congregation as an "ad hoc pastor." As at Wesley Woods, I felt honored to hear their stories, but I also felt very weary. So when people on my visiting list passed away one by one, I didn't request new names, making fewer and fewer visits over time.

In Atlanta my identity had been anchored in my role in the church. I was a young "up and coming" pastor, enjoying the respect of my parishioners, seminary professors, ministerial colleagues, and leaders of the Greater Atlanta Presbytery. My friends there knew who I had been before my brain injury. All of that was lost in Asheville. I felt known only as a "broken" person, someone who needs help and doesn't know who she is.

It seemed I was being reminded at every moment and in every context that my life hadn't turned out at all the way I thought it would. As with most survivors of brain injury, it was marked by a distinct Before and After. In his book *Disability, Providence, and Ethics*, Dutch ethics professor Hans Reinders described brain injury well: "This sense of loss creates the gap between a past that was familiar and a future that is dreadfully uncertain, in the midst of which is the abyss of a bewildering present."[1]

Michael described my eight years in Atlanta after the accident as a time of striving to return to pastoral ministry, "followed by liminal time in Asheville marked by uncertainty." He recently summed up my first years in Asheville this way: "Your library was ruined in a flood, your hoped-for therapy dog was too mean, the clown troupe disbanded, the elders you visited for the church died, you developed chronic hand pain, and invasive weeds took over your garden." Then he added, "But no doubt you have Sparky's spirit of resilience: never give up."

I had always considered myself resilient, but I was beginning to wonder. Discouragement settled deep into my spirit. Despite Michael's confidence, I felt myself giving up. And I didn't know how to get myself back.

1. Reinders, *Disability, Providence, and Ethics*, 93.

7

Forward

Michael watched as I dropped further and further into what he called an "isolating spiral." I wasn't quite sure how to pull myself out of it, but I knew I needed to connect more deeply with others who shared challenges similar to mine.

In January of 2011, I launched my blog, which I call Noggin Notions. I saw it as one answer to my dilemma, a way of reaching out and networking. I wanted to reflect regularly on my own struggles and triumphs, as well as to write about the intersection between brain injury and theology, disappointed that I could find so little written on the subject.

In one of my earliest blogs, I described my situation this way: "I am a new creation now after my brain injury. I'm trying to give my worries and concerns to God. It sure is hard to let go of things. But this is how I am now. God will help me, and I don't need to think I have to do it all. If I mess up a few things, that's okay. God loves me anyway. I just need to have love and compassion for myself."

I looked around for a brain injury support group. In Asheville, as in most places, such groups were organized *for* survivors but not *by* us. Michael and I wondered if we might be able to co-lead a group in which persons with brain injuries could share our stories and challenges.

In December of 2011, we started The Brainstormers Collective. We began small, borrowing space at the local Center for Independent Living and then in a church on Wednesday evenings, growing slowly over time. In addition to regularly providing an inviting and safe space for sharing and listening, we participated in a walk-a-thon to raise money for the Brain Injury Association of North Carolina and in some educational events to raise awareness. From the beginning, we wanted to be involved in advocacy on behalf of brain injury survivors.

One of our most transformative efforts was being part of the Unmasking Brain Injury project. Creating masks as a form of art therapy was first used at the Walter Reed National Military Medical Center in Bethesda, Maryland, with veterans who had sustained traumatic brain injuries, mostly from close encounters with IEDs (improvised explosive devices) in Iraq and Afghanistan. Many didn't know how to talk about their experience and suffered in silence, afraid or embarrassed to ask for help.

When handed a blank, white mask, an array of paints and adornments, and instructions to create a work of art expressing their feelings, not everyone jumped at the chance. Staff Sgt. Perry Hopman, who served as a flight medic in Iraq, admitted that he thought it was a joke. He said, "I wanted no part of it because, number one, I'm a man, and I don't like holding a dainty little paintbrush. Number two, I'm not an artist. And number three, I'm not in kindergarten."[1]

One therapist said that when service members initially enter the art-therapy studio, their faces "often are blank and unyielding, hiding unwelcome war souvenirs within—the mental cargo they've lugged home but can't shake. On their masks, they expose that secret turmoil: vulnerabilities, anger, grief or, often, fragmented identities."[2] And that starts many veterans on the path to healing. Staff Sgt. Hopman eventually admitted that he had been wrong and that creating a mask "is what started me . . . opening up and talking about stuff and actually trying to get better."

1. Alexander, "The Invisible War on the Brain," 44.
2. "Unmasking the Agony."

The exercise was powerful for our Brainstormers group as well. It opened space for us as brain injury survivors to express our hurts and frustrations in a non-verbal way. Some of the masks that individuals created were very elaborate, using many colors and artistic touches such as feathers, sequins, and beads. Mine was quite simple. I covered it in purple paint, my favorite color. Then I added two symbols that speak to me of the nature of God. The first was a moon, which represents constant presence to me. The second was a rainbow. I've always liked the biblical story of Noah's Ark, ending with the rainbow in the sky as the sign of God's faithful covenant of protection. I needed those reminders of God's promises.

We donated our masks to Hinds' Feet Farm in Huntersville, North Carolina, a residential center and day program for survivors of brain injury that was instrumental in expanding the project beyond veterans and around the country. The staff added our masks to a national Unmasking Brain Injury traveling exhibit that has been on tour all over the United States.

The farm's founders drew its name from Habakkuk 3:19: "God, who is my strength, will make my feet like hinds' feet, and will make me walk upon high places." That verse spoke to them about God's faithfulness to all people, whatever our abilities, calling each of us to reach our highest potential.

I had no idea that an abrupt change in the political landscape would push me to reach beyond the limits I saw in myself in a way I could never have foreseen.

* * *

Just as I was beginning to more deeply understand and accept my own vulnerability, a shift in politics in North Carolina rendered hundreds of thousands of people in my state at risk. In the fall of 2012, voters elected Pat McCrory as governor and gave Republicans a majority in our General Assembly's Senate and House of Representatives, putting both the executive and legislative branches of the government under Republican control for the first time in 142 years. Behind the manipulated outcome was some slick redistricting that the US Supreme Court ultimately ruled was "racial gerrymandering" designed to benefit Republicans. This shuffling of voters was just the beginning of an avalanche of atrocious political maneuverings and legislative actions that put North Carolina on the national stage in a way that was both tragic and embarrassing.

In short order our state House passed a law repealing same-day voter registration, limiting early voting, and requiring voters to present government-issued photo IDs. This too landed in court, with the Fourth Circuit US Court of Appeals unanimously voting to overturn the law, stating that its provisions "target African Americans with almost surgical precision" and "impose cures for problems that did not exist."[3] This didn't stop the lawmakers from repealing the Racial Justice Act, which had allowed death-row inmates to challenge their sentences on the basis of racial discrimination.

The legislators were just getting started. In our state ranked forty-first in teacher pay and forty-third in per-pupil spending—where public school teachers were earning on average $9,500 less than the national norm—the governor and legislators denied teachers raises and tenure and cut out of the budget $120 million for teachers' assistants. With the nation's fifth-highest unemployment rate, North Carolinians watched our elected officials cut unemployment benefits by 35 percent and reduce the maximum weeks of assistance by almost half, thus disqualifying 170,000 out-of-work citizens from receiving federal benefits. They proposed tax cuts for the rich, weakened environmental protections, and—wildly asserting a connection to combatting the imposition of Islamic Sharia law on our state—restricted access to abortion.

Just when we thought it couldn't get any worse, along came House Bill 2—more commonly known as "the bathroom bill." Opponents have called it the most anti-LGBTQ legislation in the United States. The part of the law requiring transgender persons to use public restrooms that correspond with the gender on their birth certificates received the most attention, but the bill also

3. Blythe, "4th U.S. Circuit."

prevents cities from enacting anti-discrimination policies and setting a local minimum wage. Once again the courts were visited, as the ACLU (American Civil Liberties Union) and the US Department of Justice brought lawsuits, answered by a countersuit from Governor McCrory himself. Only economic pressure as a result of travel bans from numerous states and cities, and a boycott of North Carolina by musicians, sports franchises, and the film industry, brought a partial repeal of this absurd and abhorrent bill.

Perhaps most reprehensible of all, the lawmakers opted out of the Affordable Care Act's (ACA) Medicaid expansion, refusing tens of billions of federal healthcare dollars and denying medical coverage to half a million low-income and/or disabled North Carolinians. According to *The Charlotte Observer*, as many as 1,145 unnecessary deaths per year in our state have been the result of people being unable to afford routine tests, medications, and treatment.[4] As far as I can tell, pure meanness and a spiteful commitment to undermining the ACA, often called "Obamacare," were behind this cruel decision.

* * *

Vulnerability had become the bedrock policy on which our state runs, consigning more and more North Carolinians to marginalization and desperation. A growing multitude of people decided they weren't going to stand for it. Leading the charge was Rev. Dr. William Barber, then head of the North Carolina chapter of the NAACP. On April 29, 2013, he and a throng of protesters launched the Moral Mondays movement at the Capitol building in Raleigh. In his speech that day Rev. Barber explained, "We have no other choice but to assemble in the people's house where these bills are being presented, argued, and voted upon, in hopes that God will move in the hearts of our legislators, as He moved in the heart of Pharaoh to let His people go." Seventeen people were arrested for refusing to leave the Capitol, as hundreds watched in support. The numbers grew rapidly from there.

4. Nichol, "Poor die without N.C. Medicaid expansion."

I became increasingly astounded and outraged at our out-of-control legislature and followed the protests closely. I was particularly moved when a group of clergy were arrested on June 10, 2013. I so very much wanted to be among them.

I knew that because of my brain injury, it would be too difficult for me to participate. Raleigh is a four-hour drive from Asheville, and the travel alone would be challenging enough. Jail is noisy, and the arrestees typically weren't being released until two or three o'clock in the morning. Still, I couldn't let go of my desire to be part of it.

I was on my way to a haircut appointment one afternoon, walking up Haywood Street, the main thoroughfare through my busy West Asheville neighborhood, pondering how to make it work. The traffic was loud and overwhelming. The hair salon offered no respite, as pounding music was playing there. I struggled to filter it out as I sat in the chair. The experience exhausted and reminded me why it was best for me not to get arrested in Raleigh.

But then I talked with some people who had been through the experience to get a better idea of what I would be getting into if I participated. I consulted with several friends, who understood the challenges but offered encouragement. I'm pretty sure Michael got tired of my agonizing about it for days.

Though my brain injury has rendered me vulnerable in significant ways, I am acutely aware that I have benefited from good health insurance, a spouse with a job, church and governmental disability assistance, a level of education helpful for navigating the complexities of the medical system and my recovery, and the privileges accorded those of us with white skin. I would not be functioning as I am without the top-notch medical, diagnostic, and rehabilitation care I received. I might not even be alive.

Mike, the son of my friend Leslie Boyd, was denied a colonoscopy because he couldn't afford to pay for it. While he waited for three years for assistance from Medicaid, colon cancer ravaged his body. He died in 2008 at the age of thirty-three. Nine days later Leslie learned that he had finally been approved for Medicaid when his first benefit check appeared. Leslie became very active in the Moral Mondays movement. She even designed a T-shirt with the slogan "Jailed for Justice" for those who were arrested.

I knew it would be a stretch to make it through an arrest, but I couldn't seem to get the idea out of my head. I wondered if I was hearing God's voice, or my own. I didn't know. It was one of those moments when I wished that God would simply take away my brain injury. But I knew God wasn't going to do that, believing that God doesn't remove our struggles but gives us ways to get through them—and God had already seen me through a lot.

Finally, when my friend LisaRose Barnes agreed to drive me to Raleigh and accompany me throughout the experience, I decided I had to do it. I wondered several times, am I making a mistake? Perhaps. But I told myself that I could simply step out of the line when the protesters entered the Capitol if I thought it would be too much stimulation for me. I could even leave the building if my compensatory strategies didn't work.

But that was hard for me to consider. I don't do well in situations where I have to think on my feet, because my brain processes information slowly and it takes me a while to make a decision. I like to have everything figured out beforehand. But it's pretty impossible to plan how a protest action is going to go.

A friend reminded me that, if I decided not to go forward, it doesn't mean I'm a failure. It just means I'm not able to do this now, and I can support the protest in other ways. Her words were helpful, because my brain injury often makes me feel like a failure. And for a time I believed that only people willing to get arrested are true activists and that, until I had that experience, I wasn't one of them. I've changed my tune drastically on that. All of us have our own ways of contributing to the cause of justice.

Risking arrest on behalf of justice is usually called "civil disobedience." But I remembered hearing around the Open Door Community in Atlanta that a better term would be "divine obedience," and I liked that. Dr. Martin Luther King Jr. was right when he said that unjust laws must be challenged and broken; that God's higher law is the one Christians must follow.

I was also inspired by a wonderful report by former Duke Divinity School professor Willie James Jennings about his Moral Monday arrest. He wrote, "The modern lie of individualism is most powerful when we imagine that boldness comes from within. It does not. It comes from without, from the Spirit of God."[5] I felt God's Spirit with me, especially through the many people who listened to my fears and offered me their wisdom.

* * *

The rally on Monday, June 24, 2013, was packed, with people everywhere. I was extremely grateful that LisaRose brought me and stayed by my side, helping me navigate the huge crowd and loud noises, which seemed almost unbearable at times. During most of the speeches, I sat off to the side on a ledge, eyes closed, neon-pink ear plugs in, resting my brain—having long before gotten over feeling silly about doing so in public.

Those of us who were planning to enter the Capitol and risk arrest were summoned to the front. We led the march into the legislature building lobby. I gathered my courage and joined others in speaking a few words about why I had decided to participate in the action. I had my brief statement written on index cards, and I was glad to be able to talk about my brain injury and my commitment to take a stand on behalf of others who also feel vulnerable. Before the marchers who were not risking arrest left, I ended up standing with Rev. Barber and James Andrews, president of the AFL-CIO, as all of us in the crowd sang "Solidarity Together."

When the handcuffs closed around my wrists, I was well aware that my ear plugs were in my pocket, out of reach, and would have to stay there. At the jail, I was put in a holding cell with ten other women. We immediately went around the circle sharing our names and our history with civil disobedience. For many of us, including a woman who was eighty-two years old, this was our first arrest.

5. Jennings, "Becoming the Common."

We were moved to a large room for processing, which took hours. As luck would have it, during the seemingly endless stretch while I was waiting for my turn, I was seated next to a woman who had done many actions and knew how to sing during them. She led us in song . . . after song . . . after song. So much for resting my brain.

When we were set free just before 10 o'clock that night, State Senator Earline Parmon was waiting outside to warmly greet and thank each of us. I was relieved that it wasn't the early-morning release I was expecting. I had the thought then that maybe in five years, with my brain function getting better and better as time goes on, I might be able to spend an entire night in jail. But when I recalled the challenges of visiting Terry Mincey on death row in Georgia, I wasn't sure.

I was fined a hundred dollars and ordered to do twenty hours of community service. I remembered how often activists I know have said that they feel like they're being sentenced to carry on with their lives when they get community service. That felt true for me, too. I was still making a few pastoral visits to elderly members of Grace Covenant and volunteering with our Saturday Sanctuary program, which provided respite and a safe space for people living on the streets. So the pastor, Mark Ramsey, signed off on my fulfillment of my sentence.

A total of 924 people were arrested in Raleigh during the 2013 protests, drawing critical public attention to the unjust laws emanating from our Statehouse. On August 5 of that year, 10,000 people gathered outside the courthouse in Asheville for the first Mountain Moral Monday. I again got to experience the powerful preaching of Rev. Barber and to participate in the passionate chant that had emerged as the motto of the movement: "Forward together, not one step back!"

In January 2014 the Moral Mondays movement spread to Georgia. That month also saw the launch of Truthful Tuesdays in South Carolina. In the years since, Moral Monday events have taken place in several other states, including Florida, Alabama, Missouri, Illinois, Indiana, and New Mexico. Rev. Barber, who in

2017 helped to resurrect the Poor People's Campaign calling for a national moral revival, has crisscrossed the country providing training and sharing lessons learned. This incredible groundswell for justice started right here in North Carolina, and I'm glad to be a small part of it. Our state may be known for some atrocious laws, but we're also now known for some amazing resistance to them.

The cruelty, exclusion, and disdain that have been our lot on the state level are multiplying in our national policies since the last presidential election. The divisions between us are creating a deepening chasm, and an ever-widening net of enmity threatens African Americans, Muslims, immigrants, women, LGBTQ persons, and other vulnerable souls.

On June 25, 2017, in the thick of debate about healthcare reform, Republican Senator Ron Johnson of Wisconsin compared people with chronic illnesses and disabilities to irresponsible drivers and damaged cars. He declared on *Meet the Press* that health insurance companies should not be forced to provide coverage to people with preexisting conditions, since we don't "require auto insurance companies to sell a policy to somebody after they crashed their car."[6] Protests erupted around the country, and many members of the disability-rights activist group ADAPT were arrested. Images of some in wheelchairs being forcibly removed from them and carried off by police swept through social media, causing outrage in many quarters.

Because it was so difficult, my "divine obedience" in Raleigh may be my only arrest. I feel called primarily to do the quiet work of being present with homeless friends and, most recently, helping to establish places of sanctuary for undocumented neighbors threatened with deportation. But difficult times call for bold and sacrificial responses. Who can know what God might call us to in the future?

"Forward together, not one step back!"

---

6. Thompson, "GOP senator."

8

Crash

Soon after my Moral Monday arrest, I discovered another an-swer to prayer. In July 2013 I attended the Summer Institute on Theology and Disability in Toronto. The Institute was launched in 2010 with a grant from the Pennsylvania Developmental Disabilities Council as part of a clergy training project. It is now affiliated with the Collaborative on Faith and Disability, formed in 2012 with a mission to support persons with disabilities and their families and allies by providing leadership in research, education, and service. Meeting annually in different cities, the week-long Institute brings together persons with disabilities, theologians, scholars, and faith leaders to share insights, offer mutual support, and explore the gifts and needs of persons with disabilities.

The fact that I went to Canada without Michael, who wasn't able to go with me, speaks to the depth of my desire to be there. Traveling is difficult for me. Airports bombard me with over-stim-ulation, and details become mind-boggling. Leaving my familiar environment is always nerve-wracking, and on top of that, I had never traveled outside the US before. I went a couple days early to give myself plenty of time to get oriented to the new setting.

The layout of the airport, my spatial orientation challenges, and the preponderance of French being spoken made arriving in Toronto a nightmare for me. Bill Gaventa, the director of the

Summer Institute, was at the airport at the same time. We had decided to meet there, but I was too disoriented to be helpful to our connecting. We talked by cellphone, and he finally said, "Tell me where you are and I'll meet you there." Completely overwhelmed, I found a chair, put in my ear plugs, closed my eyes, and waited.

The trip to the conference site took longer than expected, and by the time we arrived I was exhausted. *It's okay*, I thought. *I'll be fine after a good night's sleep.* No such luck. Participants were staying in a university dormitory. My room was on the eighteenth floor, right behind the elevator, and I heard it all night long going up and down, up and down. Even my ear plugs didn't block out the noise. And my room was sweltering.

Realizing that if I stayed there for the whole week I would be a wreck, I requested and was reassigned a room with a working air conditioner away from the elevator. *I still have a day to rest and get oriented*, I assured myself. I felt better after a little rest, but every ride in the elevator was a packed encounter with chattering students, and finding my way around the campus was extremely difficult.

Despite the challenges, I loved the Institute, where I felt like a kid in a candy store. I met theologians and pastors, people with and without disabilities, others who like me were attempting to understand disability from a faith perspective. There, I was respected and valued for my opinions because I have a disability, which isn't usually the case in other environments.

After each presenter finished, the floor was opened for questions and comments. Individuals with a range of vocal abilities spoke. The presenters waited until each respondent finished. I thought of the numerous workshops I've attended in which speakers grew impatient with persons who spoke slowly. But at this conference many of the most thought-provoking questions and insights came from such folks. The presenters all modeled a different, sensitive response, taking time to truly listen.

I didn't want to miss anything, so I took it all in. I was in a big city, in another country, away from my usual support system, and unable to retreat regularly to quiet space. As the week progressed, managing my cognitive overload started to feel overwhelming. Bill noticed that I was struggling and graciously organized a "circle of support": three people who checked in regularly with me. But, still, I pushed myself beyond my limits. And, though I had allowed myself to become overstimulated in other settings, for the first time I experienced losing control.

When a field trip to Daybreak was announced for Wednesday evening, I signed up to visit this community in the L'Arche tradition, a loving home for persons with intellectual disabilities. I skipped that afternoon's presentations so that I would have energy for the trip. But that night did me in. The two-hour drive there, the traffic jams, and the conversations were all too much. On the way home I was so weary that I stretched out on the bus seat and fell asleep.

The next couple of days are a blur, but I remember I couldn't sleep and spent time at night roaming the halls. It was like I was in a trance of some sort. I called Bill in the middle of Thursday night, about 2 AM. He threw a pair of jeans over his pajamas and met me in the hallway. Maybe it's best that I don't remember what I was wearing. I wasn't thinking clearly and have no idea what I said, but I was worried about Michael back home in Asheville. Bill offered some reassuring words, and I went back to my room and tried, unsuccessfully, to sleep.

On Friday morning I was so exhausted after I ate breakfast that I lay down and fell asleep underneath the cafeteria table, not caring what anybody thought. I began seeing people from Asheville who definitely were not there. I was convinced that Michael had died. When I called him at his office, I was so out of it that I thought he was in the hospital—even when he put his boss on the phone to assure me that he was fine. I even called Nancy Hastings Sehested, one of my pastors at Circle of Mercy, to have her check on Michael, telling her that he had had a heart attack. I believed that everyone was lying to me.

What happened next I know only from what people described to me later. The Institute was ending that day, and Bill was very concerned about my flying home alone. He found someone to be with me on the flight to Charlotte, but I refused to go to a clinic for an evaluation so that Air Canada would accept my need for accompaniment. As Bill tried to work out the details of the dilemma on the phone with Michael, the clinic, and the airline, I drifted away. A campus security guard discovered me, wandering without shoes in the observatory on the top floor of the dorm.

Still believing that people were lying to me, I apparently told this tall, burly guard, "I'm going to go down there and keep yelling at them until they listen to me!" Then I took a swing at him. He restrained me and called the police. Bill reappeared about the same time the officers arrived. I thought Bill was dangerous and the police were there to protect me from him. I objected vehemently when they put handcuffs on me. When Bill tried to get in the elevator with us, I threw a fit. He knew immediately that it would be best if he stayed behind and caught up with me later.

Bill had arranged for me to be evaluated at Mt. Sinai Hospital in the heart of downtown Toronto, and in my confusion I wondered, *How did I end up in Israel?* Amazingly, I was admitted with no ID, no money, no insurance card—and no shoes. I was taken to a quiet room in a holding area and given medication to calm me. And then I was moved to the observation unit of a psychiatric facility, where I slept for a day and a half.

The admitting psychiatrist at the hospital had called Michael, and they spoke about my condition. But when I was sent to the psychiatric facility, confidentiality protocol went into effect and Michael was unable to get further information about my status—not even confirmation that I was there.

As someone working in the mental health field in the US, Michael feared drug cocktails or worse being administered to me, but he was powerless to influence my treatment. Fortunately, none of his fears came true. Very concerned about me—and aware that the police had contacted the airport to alert personnel there that I was prohibited from flying alone—Michael got on a plane on Saturday morning and flew from Asheville to Toronto, so that I could be released into his care when I was ready.

When I eventually woke up, I became aware of my situation: I was trapped in a hospital in Canada until my husband came to set me free. I called Michael's cellphone and was worried when he didn't answer. I frantically dialed Mark Ramsey, the pastor of Grace Covenant back in Asheville, and he didn't answer, either. I began to panic, thinking, *Oh no! No one knows where I am. I'm stuck here for the rest of my life!*

People with brain injuries can have a tendency to catastrophize.

Michael showed up on Sunday. I was released, still without shoes, and we went back to the dorm to gather my things and then flew home. The harrowing experience shook me up, sending me into a deep depression. Confusion lingered for several months, and recovery came slowly.

But I remained extraordinarily grateful for the Summer Institute on Theology and Disability. Being there validated my struggles, placing my brain injury challenges in the context of Christian theology, academic knowledge, and compassionate community. The amazing leadership demonstrated by Bill Gaventa and others in Toronto offered a real-life slice of the vision that grounds the Institute's work.

In the aftermath, Michael and I had a phone conversation with Bill. When Michael asked him how he could possibly set aside his enormous responsibilities managing the Institute to spend so much time personally supporting me, Bill said simply that it would all be meaningless if he didn't "walk the talk."

The following summer, Michael went with me to the 2014 Summer Institute in Dallas as my "attendant." I don't care for the term, but I certainly didn't want to repeat Toronto, and it enabled him to accompany me without having to pay the full registration fee. I made the most of it, teasing him about "attending" to my needs by getting me breakfast in bed during the Institute. He refused to cooperate.

Since then I've been introduced to the term "care partner" by people working with individuals who have Alzheimer's disease. I prefer it over "attendant" or "caregiver." Michael is my husband, not my caregiver. And care partner is a much more respectful description for an adult who needs some assistance. Which—on a deeper level than ever before—I had to face and accept was true for me.

* * *

Re-engaging with theology at the Summer Institutes brought me new life. I loved immersing myself again in Scripture and wrestling with theological truths. I'm particularly grateful for a few insights that helped me to understand and embrace more fully my disability and my limitations.

I had continued to be tripped up by the biblical healing passages such as Isaiah's post-exilic vision that "the blind would see, the deaf would hear, the lame would leap and the speechless would sing for joy." Like many preachers, I had come to believe that interpreting such images about transformed bodies metaphorically is less offensive than taking them literally. So, for example, God wants to heal the "blindness" of those who don't see injustice and oppression, the "deafness" of those who ignore the cries of those who suffer, and the "paralysis" of those who refuse to act.

I'm grateful to Kathy Black, a United Methodist pastor, professor at the School of Theology at Claremont, and the author of *A Healing Homiletic: Preaching and Disability*, who pointed out the flaw in this way of thinking. Her reflections got me pondering. How would I feel if my disability were equated with moral failure? In our churches, disabilities have become convenient and acceptable images for negative realities such as ignorance, apathy, and hardheartedness. That's hardly fair to those of us who live with them.

More clarity came when I heard a stunning speech by ethicist and rabbi Julia Watts Belser at the Summer Institute in Atlanta in 2015. She had first delivered it on March 25 that year, as the inaugural Nancy Eiesland Memorial Endowment Lecture at Emory University's Candler School of Theology. Watts Belser deepened my understanding of Isaiah's promise.

In Isaiah's world—as in many places today—disability is frequently a product of war, conquest, and oppression. Soldiers are maimed. Enslaved persons are mutilated with marks of ownership. Overworked laborers are disabled when backs are overburdened, limbs are broken, or eyes are strained—from Pharaoh's enslaved builders to today's children abused in sweatshops and farmworkers exploited in pesticide-laden fields. Starving, impoverished bodies under siege bear the scars of the brutal incursions of empire.

This is the context in which Isaiah's transforming imagery and Jesus' healing power brought good news. For folks living in exile or under occupation, healing is resistance. Healing is rebellion—a claiming of a power stronger than imperial power.

Watts Belser acknowledged that healing can be a powerful expression of religious promise. "But," she said, "the *imperative* to be healed—the assumption that disabled bodies and minds all desire and require healing—functions as a form of violence and a kind of imperialism. [It] assumes that 'able' bodies and minds are so obviously and naturally desirable that everyone should have them, that everyone should want them, that there is, in fact, no other dignified way to live."[1] Particularly for those of us who have sustained brain injuries for which there is no "cure," living in a culture obsessed with medical solutions and technological fixes, this is an oppressive truth.

Nancy Eiesland made the point in *The Disabled God* that the greatest obstacles persons with disabilities face are not the result of bodily impairment but of societal prejudice and stigmatization. She advocated changing the attitudes, relations, and institutions that segregate and marginalize "nonconventional bodies." Disability activists are challenging ableism: the idea that all of us should have bodies and minds that match an able-bodied norm—and that those of us who don't are flawed or incomplete. Disability is not a tragic deviation from what's acceptable, needing to be "fixed." It offers a different, but important and often creative way of being in the world.

---

1. Watts Belser, "Violence, Disability, and the Politics of Healing."

John Swinton, director of the Centre for Spirituality, Health and Disability at the University of Aberdeen, Scotland—and an engaging Summer Institute faculty member—wrote the introduction to *Living Gently in a Violent World: The Prophetic Witness of Weakness*, a book of essays by Stanley Hauerwas of Duke Divinity School and L'Arche founder Jean Vanier. Swinton described being a chaplain in a facility for people with various forms of mental illness and intellectual disabilities. He said that he wasn't interested in diagnoses. "What did interest me," he wrote, "was how people with these life experiences viewed the world. They saw things differently. And when I listened carefully, those whom the world called 'mad' or 'disabled' became a conduit that allowed me—and anyone else who chose to look and listen—to receive a different truth in the midst of a world that loves to deceive."[2]

When I read that, I remembered a moment when I was a member of the Emory Brain Injury Support Group in Atlanta. It was one of the few places where I felt free be honest about myself and my weaknesses. It didn't matter if I forgot someone's name multiple times, because other brain injury survivors there did the same thing.

One day a conflict erupted in the group. People were angry, with several speaking at once. I had a hard time following the discussion. Brian, who used a wheelchair and whose speech was difficult to understand, finally shouted "Stop!" After a pause, with great deliberation he continued, "We . . . are . . . all . . . on . . . the . . . same . . . side!"

Silence filled the room. Everyone knew he was right. Brian spoke the truth. From the one who struggled the most to articulate his thoughts came the prophetic word.

2. Hauerwas and Vanier, *Living Gently*, 10.

9

Vulnerability

On the afternoon of Friday, June 2, 2017, I was in a flurry of activity, getting ready for that year's Summer Institute on Theology and Disability, which was gathering at Azusa Pacific University near Los Angeles, California. I had a long to-do list. I got a haircut. I went to the grocery store to pick up snacks for the flight. I stood in a long line at the post office to mail a package, taking deep breaths, only to discover when I got up to the window that I hadn't filled out the paperwork I needed.

People behind me were obviously annoyed, as were drivers on the road that day when I drove the speed limit and they wanted to go faster. I experience this reaction a lot, and I try to ignore it. Everybody's in such a rush these days. In the car I put on a classical violin CD, and between errands I took slow whiffs of the sandalwood-tinged essential oil I keep in my purse, to try to stay relaxed. Clearly, I was beginning to feel the stress of a big trip.

I think I recognized my calling that afternoon. As I was driving, the phrase came to me that I'm a "minister of vulnerability." As such, I can be as slow as I need to be. I don't have to keep up with everybody else, and there's freedom in that. In our fast-paced, competitive, cutthroat society, it generally isn't safe or respectable to be vulnerable. But I have nothing to lose, so I might as well be honest with myself and others. And in slowing my pace and showing my weakness, I can open space for others to share the tender and fragile places inside them.

I liked the idea of being a minister of vulnerability. In fact I was so excited about it that I stopped in a parking lot and sent off an email to Joyce Hollyday, with a description of my afternoon and my newfound understanding of my calling.

I also included some changes in the workshop that she and I were going to co-lead the following Tuesday afternoon at the Summer Institute. Based largely on learnings we gleaned from writing this book together, we had titled it "Forgetting the Former Things: Brain Injury and Vulnerability." Though I had struggled over the previous weeks to come up with what I wanted to share, my mind had clicked into gear and was racing, generating a flood of ideas just twelve hours before I had to leave.

Joyce too was preparing for the trip, but she took time to incorporate my last-minute additions into our workshop presentation. That evening when I read over the new version, I felt excited about what we were going to share. I was able then to focus on my packing. It took a while, but when I finished I got a burst of energy and couldn't sit still. Instead of going to bed, I stayed up and cleaned the house.

Around midnight a weary Michael got up and said, "Tamara, you really need to get to bed. We have to leave early in the morning."

Still frenetic, I shouted at him, "Leave me alone! I don't want to come home to a dirty house!" Michael knows that having a clean house has never been a top priority for me, but he also understands that when I get demanding like that, there is nothing he can do. He turned around and went back to sleep. Finally, around one o'clock in the morning, I stopped cleaning and joined him. Four hours later, my alarm rang. I dragged myself out of bed, and we left for the airport.

I was a mess—tired, ornery, and not much fun to be around. I slept on the forty-five-minute flight from Asheville to Atlanta. Then I walked behind Michael as we navigated through the world's busiest airport to our gate, focusing on his back and trying to block out all the noise and lights and people rushing around me. Once we got on the plane, I settled back and closed my eyes for the entire three-and-a-half-hour flight to Los Angeles. I wasn't really asleep, but in a sleep-like state. It felt a little like being in a dark cave, hearing all the sounds around me but paying no attention to them.

It was 11 AM California time when we landed at LAX—only the fourth busiest airport in the world. We threaded our way through the crush and bustle to our rental car. Check-in wasn't until three o'clock at the dorm on the Azusa Pacific campus where we were staying, so Michael suggested that we go to the beach. He loves water, and since all I planned to do was sleep, I agreed.

We looked for a lunch place, but we got distracted and didn't eat—though we did manage to buy a couple of beach towels. As soon as we sat down on our towels by the ocean, I realized it wasn't a good idea for me to be there. After a while I returned to the car and put in my ear plugs, leaving Michael on the beach. About an hour later he came back to the car and we headed to the Summer Institute as planned.

All of that sounds simple enough, but it was way too much stimulation for me. The combination of long travel, airport chaos, jet lag, and lack of both sleep and food spaced me out. It's not easy to describe, but I just wasn't present to what was going on around me.

The Institute wasn't starting until Monday morning. Following our pattern, Michael and I had arrived two days early to give me time to get oriented and rest up for the week ahead. We pretty much had the dorm to ourselves, except for a few Institute faculty members. We went out for dinner and afterward discovered a flat tire on the car. Michael had to replace it with the under-sized spare. I was exhausted and just wanted to go back to our room.

This is when I began losing touch with reality. When we returned to the dorm, I felt hot in the room. The thermostat indicated that the battery was low, and I feared that the air conditioning would cut off in the middle of the night. We took the elevator back down to the registration desk and requested another room. That room had issues, too—the sink tap wouldn't turn off at one point, and the shower didn't work well. Nonetheless, we decided it was best to stay put and settle in. But I couldn't get to sleep. Not wanting to be by myself, I crawled out of my twin bed and crept into Michael's.

* * *

As with the Toronto episode, the rest is mostly a blur and much of what I know about what happened next I learned from the people who experienced it with me. At 5:16 on Sunday morning, Michael sent a text to Joyce, who was also in California a couple days early, visiting friends in nearby Pasadena. "We're in trouble," it began. Michael explained that I had been awake off and on throughout the night and had finally gone back to sleep—and that I was "losing [my] grip on reality."

Once the sun was up, Michael and Joyce talked by phone, and Joyce decided immediately to come to the dorm. I was wandering around in the lobby, hungry. Bill Gaventa also arrived and asked what I wanted to eat. "An omelet," I told him, "without meat." I was still in touch with reality enough to remember being a vegetarian. Bill drove to a nearby café and returned with a large vegetable omelet. But, insisting that the pieces of tomato in it were meat, I pushed it away, saying in a disgusted tone, "I can't eat this!"

I also refused to eat any of the oranges Bill had bought or anything out of the lobby's vending machines. I was greatly vexed that they didn't carry my favorite brand of soda—only its rival. I had a bag of cashews in my hand, but I didn't eat those, either. Instead, I used a couple as ear plugs for a few minutes and then put them back in the bag. When I later offered some cashews to Joyce, she said politely with a smile, "No thank you."

Michael, Joyce, and Bill tried to persuade me to get on the elevator and go back upstairs and lie down. When that didn't work, they tried to convince me to let them take me to a quiet place where I could rest. They were well aware that a voluntary admission to a facility would be far easier and quicker than an involuntary committal, which would likely come with a difficult public scene. While Michael made a few calls to locate a mental health facility, Bill pulled his car up close to the dorm and Joyce walked me to it. But, protesting vigorously, I refused to get in.

Michael decided to call the local Mobile Crisis Unit. By then it was about noon. He had to make multiple other calls to work out arrangements regarding location, timing, and insurance. I walked outside onto the campus quad. Joyce followed me. I told her I was hungry but still refused to eat. I complained about being thirsty but wouldn't drink from the water bottle in my hand or take anything she offered. I kept dodging behind bushes, saying that I was going to pee there (though thankfully I didn't), ignoring her when she encouraged me to go inside and use a restroom. I did some silly antics with my baseball cap, and at one point I attempted to commandeer a campus golf cart and drive away in it.

The brain is really amazing. Whereas some people with brain injuries get mean and violent when they push too far, I get mostly punchy and spacey and silly—which I much prefer, I guess. I regret that I did, however, say a few mean things to Joyce, as well as to Michael and Bill. There's no rhyme or reason to what someone says or does while in that state, no hidden "true feelings" surfacing in the words that get said.

What they didn't know was that I was convinced that I was a subject in a study that Ben Conner was conducting. I believed that Ben—a professor of practical theology at Western Theological Seminary in Holland, Michigan—was trying out a new technique in rehabilitation therapy. Going beyond an accepted therapeutic method of encouraging persons with brain injuries to push their limits lightly, he was having his subjects push well beyond their limits—to see if that would help them recover more quickly.

Ben was an ironic choice for director of this study that my brain invented. A year before, the 2016 Institute had been held at Western Theological Seminary, and Ben had very kindly opened his office during the week as a quiet space for me when I needed to rest. He is not the sort of person to push people mercilessly. But, believing that I was the first person in his study, I felt that it was critical for me not to eat, drink, or use the restroom, so that I could be a model participant.

A few times during the afternoon I turned around, faced Joyce and yelled, "Stop following me!" When that didn't work, I got creative, glancing and pointing at my watch several times, announcing, "Oh, look what time it is. Don't you have an appointment?" Or, alternatively, telling her that I had to be somewhere, smiling at her, waving, and saying, "Okay, bye," as I strode off.

But for three hours Joyce persisted, keeping me safe and out of traffic and away from the bushes while Michael worked out the details of my treatment. And then the two of them tag-teamed for five more hours with two social workers from the Mobile Crisis Unit. When the social workers arrived about three o'clock, I showed them where the vending machines were and apologized for the absence of my favorite soda. Apparently I also warmly greeted all the Summer Institute participants who were arriving throughout the afternoon, opening the door for several.

But not all my responses to strangers were warm. At one point someone offered some candy to Jackson, the student handing out linens in the dorm lobby. He politely turned it down. I looked at him, confused, and said, "You're the kind of person who would eat that sort of thing; you're really *big*."

When Michael later apologized on my behalf, Jackson just said, "No, it's good. I'm on the football team and I'm trying to gain weight." Without exception, staff members of Azusa Pacific were wonderful throughout the ordeal. Worthy of special note is Officer Joseph Hernandez of campus security, who unlocked the prayer chapel especially for me, thinking that being in that space might calm me. Unfortunately, I refused to take advantage of his kindness.

* * *

As the day dragged on and I became more tired, hungry, and dehydrated, I also grew more angry and agitated. Still convinced that I was the first subject in a research project and committed to setting a good example for others, I repeated over and over, "I can do this." Michael and Joyce told me later that it was torturous to watch as I kept wandering through the dorm lobby, muttering "I'm so thirsty" and "I'm so tired," sometimes holding my head or pulling at my hair, but refusing even to sit down. They felt absolutely helpless. Joyce said she had to fight off the temptation to walk to the drugstore across the street, buy an over-the-counter sleep aid, and knock me out for a while just to give me some rest and a break from the misery.

Because I was not a danger to myself or others, I was low on the priority list, and the police and EMTs didn't arrive until eight o'clock that night. When they did, I didn't go quietly. As soon as I saw the police officers, I screamed "No. No! NO!" They tried gently reasoning with me, but I was far beyond reasoning. As they picked me up and strapped me onto the gurney, I kicked and cursed—using a crude and vulgar insult I never, *ever*, would use when I'm in my right mind. Gratefully, I remember nothing of this part—except lying on the gurney as they slid me into the ambulance, looking up and seeing the peaceful twilight sky.

All in all Michael, and later Michael and Joyce, had followed and monitored me for fourteen hours that Sunday. Utterly exhausted, and aware that there wasn't anything they could do at the hospital, they decided to stay at the dorm for the night and then visit me as soon as they could the next day. Michael was again concerned that I might be given the wrong treatment protocol, so he called the attending physician to make sure he understood that my breakdown was related to a brain injury rather than a mental illness.

At the behavioral health hospital, I was put to sleep with a mild sedative. I don't know how long I slept before I woke up and ate something. Just as in Toronto, I only needed rest to become myself again. But the difference between the two health systems was dramatic.

I received good care and nutritious meals in a quiet room in Canada without my insurance card, no questions asked, and recovered within twenty-four hours. Not having my Medicare card in California led to complications and delays, as the social workers had to confirm my coverage before I could be admitted to the hospital. The facility where I was taken was considered the best in the area, but there was little quiet there, as people loudly roamed the halls and meals were often eaten with the television blaring. When I asked an aide if it could be turned down, she nodded at the other patients and said, "Well, they're watching it." I took my plate of soggy macaroni and cheese—the only vegetarian option for lunch and dinner—and ate out in the hall.

When Michael and Joyce visited on Monday, we couldn't find a comfortable, quiet place to talk. The visitors' courtyard out back had loud rock music blasting from a boom box, and children running around screaming, and people smoking cigarettes. I begged Michael and Joyce to take me back with them. The copy I had of my intake form read, "Husband called for help because he couldn't handle her." I tried negotiating with the nurse at the front desk, pointing at Michael and explaining, "He put me here, so he can take me home."

But of course he and Joyce had to leave without me, which was as difficult for them as it was for me. On the way back to the Institute, they stopped to eat at an Indian restaurant and shared their worry and grief. Remembering Toronto, Michael feared that this would be another huge setback for me, sending me into an even deeper and longer spiral of depression. Joyce was afraid that I would abandon writing this book and give up on hope for my life. She knew how much I had prepared and looked forward to offering our workshop the next day. She said to Michael, "This is the worst thing that could happen."

* * *

I was released on Wednesday morning. I was so grateful to be out of that place and couldn't wait to re-engage with the Summer Institute and eat something other than macaroni and cheese. While Michael took care of all the paperwork, Joyce and I sat out on the hospital's front steps. I asked her to tell me everything that had happened. Every detail.

When she mentioned the cashews in my ears, the omelet, the golf cart, the bushes, I responded to each with "I remember that!" As I had learned early in my rehabilitation, I'm pretty good at getting and storing information in my brain; retrieving it is the challenge. When Joyce described what had happened, that was enough for me to remember. I apologized for what I put her through, and she assured me that no apology was necessary.

When Michael came out, we drove back to the Institute. We had missed the scheduled time for our workshop, but Bill offered us a slot on Thursday morning. We agreed to do it then—Joyce somewhat reluctantly, as she was concerned that the pressure might re-stress me. After lunch, I dictated what I wanted to share the next day with the workshop participants about my breakdown while she sat at Michael's laptop and added it into our presentation.

Michael took our new, updated version and got it printed. Then the three of us went to get dinner at the college cafeteria. Sitting between the pans of chicken Parmesan and beef stroganoff was the only vegetarian option: macaroni and cheese. We burst out laughing. That's when Joyce said she knew that everything was going to be okay.

I had no idea when we gave our workshop a subtitle about vulnerability just how vulnerable I would feel on the morning we offered it. I was grateful that it was well attended and went exactly as we had planned, beginning with a meditation on the Isaiah 43 passage with slides that Michael had put together, through my sharing and Joyce's response.

Two things stand out for me from the affirmations and reflections that participants offered after we spoke. One is an idea from Carrie Mitchell, a Presbyterian pastor serving a church near Rochester, New York. She suggested that I look into the possibility of getting my presbytery to officially authorize my vocation as a minister of vulnerability. That flooded me with hope.

The other particularly memorable point was an image that Bill shared. He had checked in on us throughout the day on Sunday when I was wandering the campus. He was moved by the sight of Joyce following me around so doggedly and thought of this verse from Psalm 23: "Surely goodness and mercy will follow me all the days of my life." This, I realized, is what we do for each other: embody God's goodness and mercy. Never giving up.

At lunch Michael, Joyce, and I reveled in our accomplishment of pulling off the workshop under challenging circumstances. I was eating a honey wheat bagel with cream cheese, which was getting stuck in my teeth. I pulled out the toothbrush I always carry in my purse, looked at Joyce, and said apologetically, "I'm going to do something really rude."

She responded, "Tamara, I can assure you that it won't be the rudest thing you've done since we got here."

We couldn't stop laughing. That's when Joyce said that she knew that not only was everything going to be okay, it was going to be great. "The worst thing that could happen" turned out to be a gift, solidifying my understanding of my calling to be a minister of vulnerability, prompting deeper understanding and reflection, opening new avenues of hope and meaning for me.

* * *

Since the trip out to Los Angeles had been overwhelming for me, Michael and I decided to do everything in our power to make the trip home less so. When we first walked into LAX, we spied an employee with several wheelchairs and asked for one. I sat down and inserted my bright pink ear plugs while Michael left to drop off our luggage.

The woman assigned to get me to our gate pushed me to the security checkpoint. As always, getting through was a nightmare for me. A TSA official even asked me to remove my eye patch so he could check it out. I walked through the body scanner and we waited for Michael. We waited and waited . . . and waited. The wheelchair attendant was clearly frustrated.

"He's opting for a body search," I explained. "He won't go through the X-ray scanner." She rolled her eyes. "That will take *forever* at this airport."

We continued to wait, and then the real fun began. She grabbed my wheelchair by the handles and announced, "Okay, we're going to the gate and he can meet us there." She was an expert at pushing that thing. She bolted off, dodging and swerving around people and getting there so quickly that, even if I hadn't been closing my eyes to reduce stimulation, I would have closed them out of fear! But we arrived safely, and she left me in a seat in the early-boarding area.

That turned out to be ironic. The gate number of our flight was changed, and everyone moved to the correct one except me, as I was too stressed to pay attention to the announcement over the loudspeaker. Michael finally caught up to me, sitting alone at the wrong gate with my ear plugs in and my eyes closed. He figured out the right one and we rushed there as fast as we could. We were the last passengers to board.

Soon after I got home, I wrote a blog about my breakdown on the trip. I began by joking, "The folks at the Summer Institute on Theology and Disability are going to quit allowing me to attend!" But in fact, that is not at all the case. It was the best possible place to have a breakdown. During that week, I was *living* what my colleagues were talking about in plenaries and workshops. From faculty members to chaplains and participants with and without disabilities, everyone showed immense understanding of my situation, and they were enormously supportive of me, as well as of Michael and Joyce. That is the gift of this gathering, and it is what draws me there year after year.

* * *

In *Living Gently in a Violent World*, Stanley Hauerwas compared people with cognitive disabilities to the canaries that miners used to carry into coal mines. The canaries, more vulnerable than the miners, collapsed whenever methane gas, which has no detectable odor, built up to a dangerous level in a mine. The miners knew to get out immediately whenever a canary keeled over.

Sometimes I feel like that canary. I've paid the price for trying to live up to the societal standard that expects us to work fast and furiously so that the competition doesn't overtake us. Being a "Type A personality," I tried for the first few years after my accident to match the pace I had kept before it. I said yes to anything asked of me, sending me into what felt like an endless spiral. I would push too hard, get cognitively overloaded, and then "keel over" and have to stay in bed for days to recuperate. As soon as I felt better, I was off and running until my body broke down again.

Many of us have given in to the cultural notion that we need to strive to be the best and accomplish the most. Being busy all the time is the normal, expected way of life in twenty-first-century North America. But Jennifer Johnson, one of my cognitive therapists, helped me to realize that my "plate" is smaller than other people's, and I need to limit what I put on it. I've lost count of the number of times that I said no to doing something because I needed to pace myself or rest, and the person who had asked me replied, "At least you have an excuse." My "excuse" is taking care of myself, which is something all of us must do. But in our society, this is considered weak—something we try to avoid at all costs.

Those of us with disabilities offer the world the gift of our vulnerability. As Michael once put it, "The vulnerable have a way of mirroring that which remains hidden in the privileged. So many people feel like they can't keep up. Even those with advanced technical degrees and decades of solid work experience feel threatened that their livelihood can be pulled out from under them any minute by automation, or corporate restructuring, or job outsourcing."

In a culture of fast food and instant communication, in which the most common complaints and a myriad of illnesses are related to busyness and stress, those of us who "can't keep up" can be teachers about slowing down and savoring life, about regular rest and Sabbath times. People with brain injuries can teach the world that it's important to take care of ourselves first. I don't mean taking this to the extreme and thinking only of oneself, but taking care of ourselves in the midst of multiple commitments to family and friends, work, volunteering, church—whatever demands our time and energy.

* * *

Even Jesus went off to spend time alone with God so that he would have the spiritual strength to continue his ministry. Even Jesus, facing an agonizing and torturous death, pleaded with God in Gethsemane to "remove this cup from me" before surrendering his will. Even Jesus had weaknesses.

I've always taken comfort in the story of his encounter with the Canaanite woman (Matt 15:21–28). Jesus was part of the Jewish culture of the first century, which had prohibitions against men talking with women and Jews mixing with foreigners. So when the Canaanite woman shouted to him, "Have mercy on me, my daughter is sick," he initially ignored her.

But the woman persisted. Her daughter needed help, and she refused to be brushed aside. Believing that his ministry was only for the people of Israel, Jesus said to her, "It isn't fair to take the children's food and throw it to the dogs." The woman had a quick retort for the implied insult: "Even the dogs eat the crumbs from the table." She helped Jesus to see the limits of his thinking and expand his mission. The Gospel of Matthew ends with Jesus' Great Commission to his disciples: "Go therefore and make disciples of *all* nations" (Matt 28:19).

The truth is, all of us have weaknesses. But we're afraid that if we show them, we'll lose our jobs, our positions, or our friends, so we try to hide them, even pretending that they aren't there. In our world, this fear is often justified. But most of us with brain injuries or other disabilities cannot practice this deception. As a result, we remind those around us that they too have weaknesses.

In a society that ranks people's value according to accomplishment and earnings, where who you are is what you do, I am no longer "competitive," or as "productive" as I once was. I need to depend more on other people. As difficult as it has been to accept that, I believe that we'd all be better off if we lived in a society that values relationship over productivity, embraces community instead of competition, and aims for the common good rather than self-sufficiency.

We're busy because it makes us feel important and valued. But we need to know that we are valued no matter what we can or can't do. God does not expect us to be busy all the time—and God's grace does not have to be earned.

Michael has spoken about "the rush to get back to normal" after our accident, "the belief that there is such a place as normal." I know many people who believe that they can figure life out once and for all, find their place in it and live there firmly until the end. But those of us with disabilities know that life is an endlessly moving target. We're always responding to uncertainty, recreating ourselves, being reshaped by the Spirit as we journey on through the wilderness to the next mountain. Along the way, we've learned a few things. And if you listen, we'll share them with you.

I learned several things from my second breakdown. One was that using a wheelchair in an airport is a great compensatory strategy. Another was that I needed to laminate my Medicare card, which I had left at home because it was flimsy and I didn't want it to rip any more. I also decided it was time to start carrying a card informing people that I have a brain injury, with contact phone numbers. I know of people who were arrested and jailed for drunkenness when they were disoriented as a result of a brain injury, and I'd like to avoid a situation like that—or worse.

After my incident in Toronto, I was too embarrassed to talk about it. This time, however, I understood completely why it happened, what it taught me, and what I felt compelled to share.

The difference was that I had Michael and Joyce with me. It was bad for all of us, but since I don't remember the worst of it, I believe the memory is harder for them than it is for me.

The frustrating part is, I know what I need to do to prevent such a crisis, and I always do—except I slipped in Toronto and Los Angeles. I pushed way too hard, which caused the breakdowns. I don't ever want Michael or others to have to go through that again, and I'm committed to doing everything I can to prevent it. But I know that, if I do slip again, support will be beside and behind and all around me when I need it.

"Surely goodness and mercy . . . "

10

Healing

I showed up at Asheville's YMCA pool with my swim cap, flip-pers, goggles, and a snorkel. I picked up a kickboard and a pull-buoy from the edge. I was ready! I'd been concentrating on my strokes, taking some lessons, trying to improve—and also working on not caring about what people thought of me arrayed in all my less-than-fashionable gear.

After I swam a few laps, a man joined me in the lane. Good pool etiquette includes letting a swimmer know you're joining them when you have to share a lane. Otherwise, it's easy to get hit with a stroke or a kick, or even to collide. And because I don't see well without my glasses, I'm especially prone to crashing into other swimmers.

I waited until we both reached the shallow end of the pool and, before I even saw his face, I said, "You know, when you start swimming in a lane it's always a good idea to let the other person know you're there." After I started speaking, I realized that he had a developmental disability. I quickly added, "Once I swam into someone and I felt horrible. I don't want you to get hurt." He nod-ded his head and then stood still.

I began swimming again. He just kept standing there, staring at me and all my paraphernalia. When I swam back, I showed him my flippers, explaining how they helped train my feet to kick better.

He followed me again then. When we got back to the deep end, he stopped, dived down, touched the bottom, and then surfaced. For a few minutes he stayed there, diving and coming up, while I kept working on my strokes, back and forth across the pool.

It occurred to me as I swam that I was relating to him as though he were a disability rather than a person. I was doing to him what people often do to me when I'm wearing my eye patch, treating me like I'm going to break or something, and not looking past the patch to see the person behind it. I decided to speak to him again, less condescendingly. I wanted to ask him how long he'd been swimming at the Y and to comment on his diving.

When I didn't see him, I asked the lifeguard about him and was disappointed to find out that he had left. I told the lifeguard I wanted to tell him I enjoyed watching him dive. "That's really nice of you," he said. He, too, was seeing a disability and not a man. I doubt that he would have considered it "nice of me" to comment on anyone else's behavior in the pool.

But I wasn't being nice. I was genuinely moved by the joy I saw on the man's face when he resurfaced after each dive to the bottom. His vulnerability freed me to see my own, and his delight helped me to get in touch with mine. He changed my attitude about swimming. I realized that I don't have to care about what other people think of me. I can still work to improve my stroke and my kick, but I don't need to be a great swimmer. I just need to love and enjoy it as much as he does.

* * *

I'm fascinated that I'm finding such freedom these days in the swimming pool. That was the one place where I felt truly like myself during my rehabilitation after the car accident. In water I moved fluidly and freely, as someone unhindered by the accident that had robbed me of so much. Part of my work of healing is discovering and learning to embrace the places and activities that bring me joy *now*. And that means letting go of other things that I once loved. "Forgetting the former things." It's excruciating work.

On a recent Sunday, two teenaged sisters played their violins in the worship service at Grace Covenant Presbyterian Church. That's the day I said to myself, "It's time." I had been aware for more than twenty years that my violin and viola need to be played frequently to continue sounding good. But ever since that humiliating moment of being barely able to scratch out a simple tune as Raindrop the clown, my violin has stayed under my bed and my viola in the closet, tucked in their cases gathering dust.

As I listened to the two young women play that Sunday, I observed their deep feeling, and I knew that I would never again experience that. Nothing can compare with how free my soul was when I played my violin. Playing seemed like the only way I could really express my emotions, and they poured out of me profusely in those days when music felt like everything.

I went home after church that day and pulled my violin and viola out of their cases. The smell of the instruments prompted a rush of memories. I remembered my nerve-wracking sixth-grade solo of the "William Tell Overture" and the stream of eager students who came to my parents' living room for lessons years later. I smiled picturing my days with the accordion-and-violin duo Bellows and Bows, conjuring again the surprised looks on the faces of patrons when my partner and I came out to play as they enjoyed their waffles and eggs. I recalled the cheap hole-in-a-wall motel I had stayed in after my only orchestra audition, and the insecurity that gripped me when I felt disappointed in my performances—as well as the exhilaration that flooded my spirit when I knew I had played well.

I believed then that nothing could ever replace the excitement, camaraderie, and merging of people's souls that happens when we're joined together playing music. But I am different now, and that particular joy is no longer available to me. Michael and others have taught me that souls can touch in other ways. And, fortunately, I can still sing. I've taken voice lessons, and even though I was more proficient on violin, I do well enough to be able to enjoy and share the gift of singing.

Prompted by an image from a sermon by author, professor, and Episcopal priest Barbara Brown Taylor, my friend David Bradley told me one evening at choir practice at Grace Covenant that he believes we each have something like a tuning fork inside us. He said that, when we sing, our whole being is in tune with the God who created us to be, and longs for us to be, ourselves. We're able then to peel away all the layers of preoccupation and concern that cloud our minds and make us forget who and whose we are.

This was what happened to me when I played my violin. If I knew a piece well, and got over worrying about playing the double stops, shifts, and arpeggios in tune, my stresses and worries disappeared and I was floating on the wings of God's Spirit. Sometimes when I sing in the choir at Grace Covenant, I reach that place where I know everyone is feeling something together. It's as if my soul becomes one with God and the people around me. It's as close as I've come to experiencing what I did when I played my violin.

So, it's time. It has taken me more than two decades, but I'm finally ready to sell my violin and viola. I'm more emotionally attached to my violin, which I named Isaac when I was a student at the conservatory—I didn't know many violinists, but I had heard of Isaac Stern. I learned in seminary that Isaac, the name the biblical matriarch Sarah gave to her late-in-life miracle son, means "he laughs." It seemed appropriate for an instrument that gave me such joy.

In the past, whenever I considered selling my instruments, I felt like I would be selling part of myself. In some ways, I guess I am. Those instruments were my heart and soul, and they will always be a part of me. But that part of my life is over, and it's time to pass them on to someone who can benefit from them—and perhaps discover the joy they once gave me.

* * *

Although I eventually came to accept that I would never again pastor a church, I missed preaching. I was grateful when I began to receive invitations to preach from time to time at Circle of Mercy and Grace Covenant. I found myself drawn back to the form of my very first sermon, the one I offered in 1990 in the chapel at Central Baptist Theological Seminary in Kansas City. I took on the voices of biblical women—not to hide or escape from my own life but to better understand it. And to share the vulnerability and strength of these sisters in faith. In losing myself for a time in their stories, I found myself in a new way, rediscovering my own story from their perspective.

My favorite is Hagar, the enslaved Egyptian woman who conceived Abraham's child when his wife Sarah could not provide him with an heir. Although this solution to their dilemma had been Sarah's idea, when it was accomplished she felt contempt toward Hagar. And when Sarah miraculously gave birth to Isaac in old age, she ordered Abraham to get rid of Hagar and her young son, Ishmael. Early one morning, Abraham sent them into the wilderness with a loaf of bread and a skin of water (Gen 21:8–21).

In my sermon offered in her voice, I attributed these words to Hagar: "I was paralyzed inside. I couldn't think, I couldn't feel, I couldn't cry. Ishmael kept asking me, 'Where are we going? Where are we going?' I did not answer him, for I did not know. We simply wandered aimlessly, with no direction and no purpose."

As time passed, the desperation of their situation sank in to Hagar: "I had no power. I had no control; I was forced out into this place. I tried to listen for Abraham and Sarah's God, but I heard only silence. A terrible, earth-shattering silence."

And then Hagar gave Ishmael the last morsel of bread and the final sip of water. "I realized that both of us were going to die. I hugged Ishmael close and I tried to stay composed. I put him next to a bush to shade him from the sun. Then I walked away. I could not bear to watch him die.

"I looked up to the sky and I wept. I wept because I had done all that I could do and it was not enough. I wept because my son did not deserve to die. I wept because I was completely alone. I wept because the God of Abraham and Sarah was so unfair and so unloving.

"And then it happened. I heard a voice call out my name. 'What troubles you, Hagar? Don't be afraid.' No one had called me Hagar in such a long time. I was just the slave woman. But this voice. This voice called me Hagar. And at that moment I knew that it was the voice of God.

"I looked around the wilderness and I saw a well of water. I got up, filled the empty skin with water, and gave my son a cup of its coolness. Colors returned. That frozen feeling was gone. Everything was different. I was no longer a slave but a woman who had survived. I was Hagar a servant of God and I knew my life would never be the same."

* * *

I don't know why some of us experience extreme rupture in our lives and are cast into a wilderness of disorientation, powerlessness, and dread. I've heard and read several brain injury survivors embrace a theology that I find troubling, making statements such as, "God caused this to happen for a reason," or "God did this to make me a better person," or "God knew there were things I needed to learn." I don't believe this for a minute. What sort of God would want lives to be ripped apart just to teach someone a lesson? What sort of God would be the cause of such suffering?

No, God doesn't cause such things to happen. The God I worship cries with me when I cry. The God I worship helps me handle whatever comes up along my journey. The God I worship is creative and brings new life.

I have found the thoughts of Rabbi Harold S. Kushner, author of *When Bad Things Happen to Good People*, very helpful. He admitted that he doesn't know why suffering takes place as it does. And he believes the better question to ask is, "This has happened to me, what do I do now?"

Hans Reinders wrote in *Disability, Providence, and Ethics* that we should not silence the "why" question, that it must be honored. But he also says that it is to a large degree unanswerable and can be paralyzing. We can learn to live with life's contingencies without despair or resignation, he wrote, only if we depend upon God's resilience and trust God's provision. God sends love into our lives to guide us in discovering "the self that finds itself at the other side of the chasm and . . . is transformed to receive a new future."[1]

Reinders lifted up stories of catastrophe being transformed into stories of hope, using as a primary example the biblical betrayal of Joseph by his jealous brothers (Gen 37:12–36). Conspiring to kill Joseph, they stole his colorful robe and threw him into a pit in the wilderness. But when they saw a camel caravan of Ishmaelites on their way to Egypt, they decided instead to make some profit and sold their brother for twenty pieces of silver.

Clearly, this was the work of men and not God. Sometimes the "why" question can be answered by taking into account human sin, greed, and cruelty.

Joseph became an interpreter of Pharaoh's dreams and rose to prominence in Egypt, saving the people from a devastating famine. God did not will that Joseph be left for dead in a pit or sold into slavery, but God transformed his suffering into good. Years later, when Joseph's brothers came to Egypt, Joseph wept loudly and revealed himself to them. He forgave them for their betrayal and brutality, telling them that although they had intended to do him harm, God had used him to save many lives and preserve a people.

We can't know for sure why some of us spend time in a pit in the wilderness. But I do know that it was in the stark and empty wilderness that our ancestors in the faith heard the voice of God as they were on their way to the Promised Land. It was there that they spent forty years being fed on manna, trusting the provision of God, learning about how to live justly and committed to the common good.

In the bleakest of landscapes and moments, God's love can lead us to courage and creativity. In the wilderness, we will be led to life-giving water. In the most difficult of places, we will be comforted. And we will be changed.

1. Reinders, *Disability, Providence, and Ethics*, 180.

The promise of Isaiah 43, which ran through my mind when I had no other thoughts after my accident, and which I repeated to myself again and again on my most difficult days, still holds:

> Do not fear,
> for I have redeemed you;
> I have called you by name,
> You are mine.
> When you pass through the
> waters, I will be with you;
> and through the rivers, they
> shall not overwhelm you;
> when you walk through fire you
> shall not be burned,
> and the flame shall not consume you . . .
>
> Do not remember the former things,
> or consider the things of old.
> I am about to do a new thing;
> now it springs forth;
> do you not perceive it?
> I will make a way in the wilderness
> and rivers in the desert.

God had guided the people of Israel into the Promised Land, but the land lost its promise when they were forced out of it. To this community in exile, Isaiah was proclaiming that even though they were far from home and things were in ruins, something new was about to happen. They had not been abandoned. They may feel thirsty and see only darkness, but ahead is a river where they can quench their thirst. They may journey in a parched wilderness of isolation and loss, but they will be carried by a flowing river of hope and grace.

Many brain injury survivors say that they would not go back to their former life, because they have so much wisdom now. I, however, would love to go back to the way I was before. Who knows where I might be? I often wonder. Perhaps I would be the pastor of a church where I would get to preach every Sunday.

Just as the exilic community longed to return home, I still want to cling to what I lost. I find it excruciatingly difficult to let it go. But, even though I sometimes feel otherwise, I know that I will be okay. That river of hope and grace still flows, and I too am being carried by it.

* * *

I have always loved Jesus' parable of the Great Banquet (Luke 14:12–24). Jesus spoke of a man who invited his friends to a huge feast. But they were all too preoccupied with their land and live-stock, their luxuries and loves, to show up for the party. So the man ordered his servant to go out into the streets and invite those described as "the poor, the crippled, the blind, and the lame"—the people with time on their hands.

This is not a picture, as I once thought, of the "unworthy dregs of society" finally making it to the table. It is a vision of the beloved of God gathered together and sharing in the earth's abun-dance, at the center of a restored and renewed community where their perspective and wisdom are welcome. It's good news flooding in from the margins.

And the margins are where Jesus chose to live his life—among the impoverished and the ill, the oppressed and the outcast. He was born there and he stayed there right to the very end, sharing the humiliation and pain of people pushed to the edges, redefin-ing power on the cross. In his emptying and surrender was his strength. In his weakness was his power.

Jesus always had time for people living on the margins—peo-ple such as the woman suffering from a twelve-year hemorrhage (Mark 5:21–34). Like her, I have sometimes felt desperate to be healed. She spent all her money on doctors and only got worse. A victim of the purity codes that declared her unclean, she was destined to live her life on the edges of society, alone, an outcast judged guilty by her body's disability. But—boldly defying the laws of the day and interrupting a man on an important mission to heal the daughter of an imposing synagogue leader—this anonymous, no-account woman reached out and touched Jesus' cloak, claiming his power to heal her.

When he felt the power flow out from him, Jesus asked who had touched him. It seemed an absurd question to his disciples, who scoffed at the idea that he should want to know who in the huge crowd around him had brushed too close. Fearful and trembling, the woman fell at his feet and told him "the whole truth." To a stranger, she made a very public confession of what had been an overwhelming personal agony. And by so doing, she rewrote her story, steering it toward a different ending.

Jesus said to her, "Daughter, your faith has made you well; go in peace and be healed." By calling her "daughter," he was acknowledging that she was part of the community. After her long and painful years of being shoved to the lonely sidelines, Jesus was declaring her place in that great throng of humanity. He did not announce that he had healed her, but instead invited her to go and "be healed." His touch was just the beginning of a process that would involve releasing her shame, reclaiming her belovedness, and finding her way into her new place.

For me, healing has meant more than accepting what is. Though my limited stamina and oversensitivity to noise and social stimulation make it frustratingly difficult, it has meant finding my way back to being part of the community. Healing has also required that I speak "the whole truth." It has meant no longer trying to hide my disability, but facing it head-on and claiming the gift of vulnerability that I have been given to share.

In that very first sermon that I preached almost three decades ago in the voice of a woman with leprosy, I attributed these words to her, as she pondered the response of one of Jesus' disciples to his command to feed the crowd: "The follower said, 'You mean you want us to go and buy food for *these* people?' I could tell what he was thinking. These people are the lowest of the low. These people are the type of people that you should ignore. These people cannot give you power. These people cannot give you anything."

Jesus blessed and miraculously fed the throng with five loaves of bread and two fish that a boy offered up. The woman ate and then thought, "I suppose if those followers were to hear our stories and understand who we are, deep inside, they would have to really look at themselves. Our blemishes are on the surface. Their hurts and soft places are where they cannot be seen. But we are much the same."

If I were given a chance to preach that sermon over again, I think I would change the ending. I would not have the woman with leprosy turn away from the fierce compassion of Jesus, or the harsh scorn of his disciples. Perhaps, like the woman with the hemorrhage, she would overcome her fear and reach out for healing, pursuing the wholeness that is hers to claim.

Such power is available to me. It is available to you, and to all of us. The catch is that we can only access it through vulnerability.

We have a choice. We can be broken down by the challenges life throws our way. Or we can be broken open to the "new thing" God is always doing, springing forth in ways beyond our imagining. If our faith teaches us anything, it's that God is a genius with surprise endings. No matter what our circumstances, there's always a reason to hope.

Bibliography

Alexander, Caroline. "The Invisible War on the Brain." *National Geographic*, February 2015, 30–53.

"Amnesty International." *Clark Prosecutor* (undated). http://www.clarkprosecutor .org/html/death/US/mincey739.htm.

Blythe, Anne. "4th U.S. Circuit Judges Overturn North Carolina's Voter ID Law." *The News & Observer*, July 29, 2016. http://www.newsobserver.com/ news/politics-government/state-politics/article92593512.html.

Connors, Susan H. "Brain Injury Association Releases Statement on TBI, Keith Lamont Scott Shooting in Charlotte." *PR Web*, September 26, 2016. http:// www.prweb.com/releases/2016/09/prweb13713544.htm.

Eiesland, Nancy. *The Disabled God: Toward a Liberatory Theology of Disability.* Nashville: Abingdon, 1994.

Hauerwas, Stanley, and Jean Vanier. *Living Gently in a Violent World: The Prophetic Witness of Weakness.* Downers Grove, IL: InterVarsity, 2008.

Jennings, Willie James. "Becoming the Common: Why I Got Arrested in North Carolina." *Religion Dispatches*, June 18, 2013. http://religiondispatches. org/becoming-the-common-why-i-got-arrested-in-north-carolina/.

Nichol, Gene. "Poor Die Without N.C. Medicaid Expansion." *The Charlotte Observer*, October 27, 2016. http//www.charlotteobserver.com/opinion/ op-ed/article110900762.html.

Rankin, Bill. "Condemned Killer's Guilt is Disputed; Mincey Lawyer Files Challenge." *Atlanta Journal-Constitution*, October 20, 2001.

Reinders, Hans. *Disability, Providence, and Ethics: Bridging Gaps, Transforming Lives.* Waco, TX: Baylor University Press, 2014.

Thompson, Annabel. "GOP Senator Compares Having a Pre-existing Condition to Crashing Your Car." *Think Progress*, June 26, 2017. www.thinkprogress.org.

"Unmasking the Agony: Art Therapy Helping Combat Veterans." *Military Veteran Project*, August 29, 2015. http://www.militaryveteranproject.org/ news/unmasking-the-agony-art-therapy-helping-combat-veterans.

Watts Belser, Julia. "Violence, Disability, and the Politics of Healing." Eiesland Endowment Lecture, Candler School of Theology, Atlanta, March 25, 2015. https://vimeo.com/123748777.